The Royal Tombs of Great Britain

THE
ROYAL TOMBS
OF
GREAT BRITAIN

An Illustrated History

AIDAN DODSON

Duckworth

First published in 2004 by
Gerald Duckworth & Co. Ltd.
90-93 Cowcross Street, London EC1M 6BF
Tel: 020 7490 7300
Fax: 020 7490 0080
inquiries@duckworth-publishers.co.uk
www.ducknet.co.uk

A catalogue record for this book is available
from the British Library

ISBN 0 7156 3310 4

Typeset by Ray Davies
Printed and bound in Great Britain by
Biddles Ltd, King's Lynn, Norfolk

Contents

Preface   vii
Introduction   1

I. The Early English Kingdoms   17

II. England   41

III. Scotland   111

IV. United Kingdom   137

Appendices   151
1. The Known Tombs of Royal Consorts   151
2. The Stuarts in Exile   162
3. Foreign Monarchs Buried in Great Britain   165
4. The Principal Chapels, Churches and Mausolea
   Containing Royal Tombs   167

Map   213
Chronology   214
Genealogy   220
Bibliography   226
Sources of Illustrations   234
Index   235

To Salima … who started it all!

Preface

The visitor to the royal chapels at Westminster, Windsor, and elsewhere, sees many tombs and memorial tablets to the deceased kings and queens of Great Britain, but is left to imagine the manner in which their bodies lie below. The general impression is that they are situated 'in the vault', but in fact there are a variety of installations. Some are indeed in what is popularly envisaged as a 'vault' – a large chamber with shelves to hold the coffins along the walls. However, some simply lie in small cavities below the floor, others in stone sarcophagi that stand in full view of the public.

Within their sarcophagus, vault or grave, royal bodies have undergone various treatments before burial. In more recent times, the closure of the lead-lined coffin has been preceded by, if anything, no more than an injection of formaldehyde, but in earlier years, other treatments took place. At one extreme, the flesh of Henry V was boiled off the bones. More generally, the internal organs were removed and the flesh treated with spices in a process akin to the Ancient Egyptian practice of mummification. As in Egypt, the removed organs were placed in a separate chest or urn that was laid at the feet of the coffin – a coffin which, down to Stuart times, would often be shaped like a wrapped human being.

Having been interred, the royal dead were not necessarily left in peace, being exhumed for religious, political or other reasons, or disturbed when the building in which they lay was rebuilt or demolished. Also, throughout the ages, antiquarians or the curious have opened a number of the tombs to examine or verify their contents. It is from these researches that much of what we know of the structure of many of the earlier graves is known. This book aims to provide a concise digest of all that has been learned from these various activities, as well as other avenues of research, to provide a rounded account of all the tombs for which details can be traced.

In spite of the apparently perennial popular fascination with royalty, published data is decidedly spotty. A comprehensive, although rather summary and occasionally inaccurate, list of royal tombs in England is given in Greenwood 1990: 19-64. Mediaeval tombs are treated in some detail in Steane 1993: 41-70, and in Duffy's superb 2003 volume, but earlier and later examples are omitted, and quite a lot of archaeological material is passed over. Bland 1986 covers royal burials since Elizabeth I, but more from their social/historical and ceremonial perspectives, and contains a number of errors concerning the tombs themselves. Some additional material is included in Litton 1991, but this covers royal material only in passing. All the foregoing effectively ignore Scottish interments. A number of nineteenth-century works exist, the most complete being Wall 1891. While containing a considerable amount of material not easily accessible elsewhere, it suffers from a number of inaccuracies, over-credibility when dealing with traditional sources and lacks any kind of bibliography or usable indication of sources. We also have Stanley 1882, which gives a fairly comprehensive account of the author's researches among the royal tombs in Westminster Abbey, albeit written (as is Wall's book) in the worst kind of flowery Victorian prose that does much to obscure necessary detail. Otherwise we seem to have only widely scattered nineteenth-century and earlier accounts of disinterments and examinations, together with a handful of modern works on particular sites, of which John Crook's works on Winchester are models of their kind.

Thus, much leg-work far from the library has been necessary, and a range of institutions and individuals deserve my thanks for their contributions to my research: The Most Reverend Archbishop of St Andrews and Edinburgh; John Burden (Surveyor of the Fabric, Westminster Abbey); Sister Margaret Connor (St Margaret's Convent, Edinburgh); John Crook (Winchester); Martin R. Davies; Frank Davies (Chairman, Kings Langley Local History & Museum Society); Enid Davies (Assistant Archivist, St George's Chapel, Windsor Castle); Don and Edna Dodson (for reading the manuscript); Mark A. Hall (Perth Museum and Art Gallery); Sheila Hilton; Bob Partridge; Elinor C. Murphy (Librarian, Shaftesbury Abbey & Museum Preservation Trust); His late Grace the 17th Duke of Norfolk; José-Ramon Pérez-Accino (for translations from the Spanish); Ken Qualmann (Winchester Museums Service); the Library of the Society of Antiquaries of London (for access to the Doyne Bell MSS, which contain many useful notes and offprints relating to British royal tombs); the Rev. Mark Tanner (Vicar of St Mary's, Wheatley); the Dean and Chapter of Westminster (for access to the material housed in the Abbey's Muniment Room); the Dean and Canons of Windsor.

Finally, my special thanks go to my wife, Dyan, for proof-reading and our many days in and around the royal cemeteries of England, Scotland, Germany and France, in weather fair and (frequently) foul, and also to my dear friend, Dr Salima Ikram, whose casual enquiry of me in St George's Chapel well over a decade ago started this whole chain of research. Salima: this is your answer!

Department of Archaeology and Anthropology, University of Bristol

Introduction

Roman rule in Great Britain ended around the beginning of the fifth century AD, and it was during the latter part of that century that the first of the dozen or so Anglo-Saxon Kingdoms came into existence. Knowledge of the posthumous fate of their kings begins to come into focus only in the seventh century. The pagan tradition is embodied in the East Anglian necropolis of Sutton Hoo, with its great mounds concealing ship burials of a type also to be seen across the North Sea. That of emerging Christianity can be seen in the churches erected by newly converted monarchs, many of which would become dynastic cemeteries. Perhaps the best example of the latter is to be seen at Winchester, where the church built by Cenewalh was the first of a series on roughly the same site that would provide the principal burial place of the kings of Wessex, and later England, for four centuries.

In Scotland, the holy isle of Iona is reputed to have received almost every one of the Scots kings down to the eleventh century, although explicit chronicles survive only in certain cases. The English kingdoms generally had one or two favoured burial places, although some kings, for the better repose of their souls, endowed anew a monastery and church to hold their bodies. The same pattern continued following English unification in the tenth century, and from the eleventh century in Scotland. Thus, while the largest proportion of interments took place respectively at Westminster and Dunfermline, many others took place in abbeys and cathedrals around the realms, some of which only ever received a single kingly burial.

After the accession of James VI of Scotland as James I of England, however, the pattern greatly simplified, with Westminster becoming, until the nineteenth century, the almost universal burial place of the monarchs of the united kingdoms. Even Lord Protector Oliver Cromwell was interred there. However, from George III onwards, the royal family's 'home town' of Windsor took over the role, and it is there that the most recent kingly burials, those of George VI and the former Edward VIII, have taken place.

However, while the broad facts of the last resting places of Britain's monarchs are clear, when one delves deeper into the detail of the story of the British royal tomb the unevenness of the evidence rapidly becomes apparent.

1. Chantry of Henry V, lying above his tomb. His wife, Catharine of Valois, was reburied in the chantry in 1878 (see p. 155).

2. Façade of Holyrood Abbey, burial place of many Scots kings.

In some cases, a king's bones can be traced over a period of some one-and-a-half millennia; in others, they are lost to sight after only a generation or two. The 'fault line' governing the survival of many royal interments comes in the sixteenth century, when the upheavals of the Reformation resulted in the destruction of many monastic establishments and, incidentally, the royal tombs housed within. Ironically, it was those monarchs who had founded new religious houses to aid their eternal repose who suffered worst from the politically inspired depredations of Henry VIII and the religiously driven ones of the Scottish Presbyterians. Thus their sepulchral abbeys were stripped of their riches and either demolished or allowed to fall into ruin, the royal monuments suffering the same fate as the rest of their furnishings.

What is most striking about this destruction is that it occurred while the descendants of the desecrated were still ruling in England and Scotland – indeed, in the latter case being of the same dynasty as the victims. In contrast, the treatment of the royal tombs during the Commonwealth was remarkably mild. Some of the mortuary chests in Winchester Cathedral were pulled down and their contents thrown around, while the tomb of Æthelred II in St Paul's was broken open, but the executed Charles I was allowed honourable burial and the tombs of Westminster and Windsor left unmolested.

Such magnanimity was not, however, shown by Charles II to Oliver Cromwell, whose body, together with those of other Commonwealth worthies buried in Westminster Abbey, was exhumed at the Restoration. Together with those of others responsible for Charles I's condemnation, Cromwell's corpse was taken to the gallows at Tyburn, hanged and then decapitated.

Against this background, this book nevertheless aims to give some account of every known burial of a ruler of Scotland, England and the latter's precursor states. In some cases, only the town of burial is known, but where other data on the tomb and interment is available they are given, together with any subsequent movements or examinations of the body. Illustrations of the monument and/or vault are also provided where possible. In addition, appendices list the burial places, where known, of royal consorts and also provide summary descriptions, illustrations and plans of the principal churches and chapels that house royal burials.

This chronicle sheds some interesting light upon the attitudes of monarchs to both their own eternal destinies and those of their predecessors. The sagas of the intended ultimate tombs of Henry VIII and Charles I (curiously enough, still sharing a vault at Windsor) say quite a lot about the relative priorities of their children, grandiose schemes coming to nought when other claims on

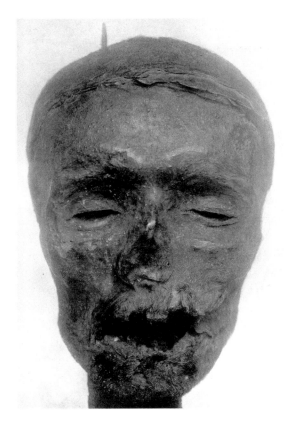

3. The embalming processes used could be remarkably efficacious. The head of Oliver Cromwell spent decades exposed on a pole above Westminster Hall (see pp. 101-2), yet retained skin, flesh and hair.

funds presented themselves. The attitudes of James VI & I are most instructively revealed in his erection of a magnificent tomb for his mother Mary Queen of Scots, whose execution he had done little to prevent, and also his own burial, not in the spacious vault in which his queen already lay, but in that of Henry VII, the ancestor on whom his claim to the English throne depended. Perhaps most touching is the case of George II. He had a double sarcophagus made for him and his wife, Caroline, and when he died, 23 years after her, instructions were left that the inner sides of their coffins should be removed so that they should lie together for eternity. To this day, the two coffin boards rest against the wall of the George II vault in Westminster Abbey.

In their modes of interment and the forms of their tombs, these various monarchs generally followed the fashions of their times. Among these fashions was the preservation of the body, a particular necessity when a king or queen might die far from home, but also highly desirable to allow lying in state, even though the body would usually be sealed inside a leaden coffin some time before its actual interment. A number of accounts survive of the process adopted, the following referring to the treatment of Edward IV:

4. The burials of most of the kings of Wessex were made at Winchester; today many of their bones lie in mortuary chests above the screens that flank the quire, together with those of some of the earlier kings of England, including Cnut (Canute) and William II.

What shall be don on the demyse of a King annoynted

When that a King annoynted is decessed, aft' his body is sp'ged, it must be washed and clensed by a bishop' for his holy annoyntemt, then the body must be bamed, wrapped in laun, or reynez yf it may be gotyn, than hosyn cherte, & a perer of shone of rede lether, & do on his surcote of cloth, his cap of estate on his hed, and then ley hym on a fair borde cou'ed with cloth of gold, his on hand on his bely & a sep'r in toder hande, & oon his face a kerchief, and so showed to his noblez by the space of ii dayes and more, yef the weder will it suffre.

And when he may not godely longer endur, take hym away and bowell hym and then eftones bame hym, wrap hym in raynez wele tramelled in cords of silke, then in tarseryn tramelled, & then in velvet, & so in clothe of gold well tramelled, and then led hym and cofre hym, & in his leed wt hym a plate of his stile, name, & the date of our Lord gravyn [...].   [Anstis] 1770

A medical textbook of a century-and-a-half later gives a more extensive account:

First of all, let the Chyrugeon make a long incision from the necke unto the lower belly; opening the breast, and taking out the heart, lungs, and others ...

After that you may show the belly inferiour, that is the stomacke and the Epipleon; considering the orifice superior and inferiour, and afterwards the bowells, bladder and other things.

All the said parts of the brest and belly inferiour being observed, must bee all cut round the Diaphragma, and cut as neere as possible can be where they are tied and taken all out, and put into a large bason or vesell. Those two bellies being emptied and cleansed, that is all the blood that cometh from the veines and Arteries dried up with Sponges: then you must come to the head.

The head or Cranium shall be sawed in two, as you doe in an Anatomie, and the braines and parts shall be put in the vessell with the bowells, together with the blood that hath been drawn out of the two bellies; that is, the head, brest and belly inferiour, and put them altogether in a barrell, and hoope it round, to be buried or put into the ground; but if they desire to carry them far, or keep them you may embalme them as followeth.

Having emptied and squeezed blood from the excrements, you must wash them in warme oxicrat, made from foure parts of water, and one of vinegar compounded …: then powder them all about with one of the balming powders …, then put them into a barrell pitcht within and without, and hoope the barrell well, and then wrappe it round with Ceare-cloth and cord it fast, then put it into a bigger barrell also pitcht and hoopt, and send it whither you please.

The head, breast, and belly inferiour being also emptied and cleansed, you shall begin to embalm them: beginning at the head being well washed within with the said vineger compounded, then with pieces of Cotten soaked with the said vineger and filled with balme, the head shall be filled, then both pieces of the skull shall bee bound together with thread.

Doe also to the brest as you doe to the head, piercing the Muscles and flesh with a bodkin, to make the blood runne out, which you must dry up with sponges, then wash and soake it with the said vineger, and fill it up with Cotten full of Balme, do so also for the belly inferiour.

The foresaid parts being embalmed, you must make long Incisions in the armes, legges, thighes, and buttocks, and principally the great veines and Arteries to make the blood runne out, and dry them up with Sponges; then soake them with the said Vineger, and stop them full of pieces of Cotten filled with Balme.

You shall then make an Incision from the shoulder to the wrist in the arme, piercing it with a bodkin to the bone all about, to make way for the blood, then dry it up with sponges, and wash and soake it well with the said vineger, and then filling it with pieces of Cotten soaked in the said vineger and filled with Balme, and then sowe it up with needle and thred, so doe to the thighes making an incision from the belly to the knee, piercing of it, and stoping and sewing of it up as before, and so the knees and others.

You may also stop the holes of the eares and nostrills and mouth with Cotten soaked in the vineger and filled with Balme.

That done, turne the corpse upon the belly and make an Incision about the Jugular veines in the necke, letting out the blood, and so make an incision down the reines, piercing the back to let out the blood, taking it away and washing it with said vineger, and fill them as before, sowing them up also the fingers and towes; incisions being made and stopped as before.

The Corps being thus embalmed shall be anointed all over with Venice Turpentine, dissolved in oyle of Roses or oyle of Spike, and then it shall bee covered all over with a Seare-cloth and put into a Coffin of Lead, the which coffin shall be filled with dry Aromaticke hearbs, as

Rue, Wormwood, Time, Scordeum, Marjoram, and others …, then cover
it and let it be well soldered.

Guibert 1639

Much of the above is borne out by modern examinations of mediaeval bodies.
The sawing of the skull to remove the brain is clearly to be seen on the head
of Oliver Cromwell, embalmed only two decades after the publication of this
treatise. This relic also attests to the efficacy of the process, as it successfully
survived exposure atop Westminster Hall, on an iron-spiked pole, for
something around a quarter-century (see pp. 5 (fig. 3), 101-2).

The evisceration of the corpse played a key role in these embalming
processes – as it had in ancient Egyptian times. From both archaeological and
literary sources, it may be seen that the disposal of the internal organs was
approached in a number of different ways. In particular, earlier kings often
had various elements of their bodies buried in different parts of their
dominions. Hearts, in particular, were placed in leaden cases, and were
frequently buried as magnificently as the body itself, sometimes including the
use of a recumbent effigy. With some later monarchs the position is unclear,
urns being absent from a number of burials, but by the latter part of the Stuart
dynasty royal coffins are almost always accompanied by their visceral chests.

In this connexion, the bill for the preparation of the body of Mary II ran as
follows:

> For perfumed sparadrape, to make cerecloth to wrap the body in, and to
> line the coffin; for rich gummes and spices, to stuff the body, and to fill
> up the urne [to hold the heart and viscera]; for Indian balsam, rectified
> spirits of wine tinctured with gummes and spices, and a stronge
> aromatised lixivium to wash the body with; for rich damask powder to
> fill the coffin, and for all other materialls for embalminge the body of the
> High and Mighty Princess Mary, Queen of England, Scotland, France
> and Ireland etc. As also for spices and damask powders to be putt
> between the two coffins, with the perfumes for the c[h]ambers;
> altogether £200 0s 0d.

Quoted in Strickland 1866, VII: 459

The eighteenth century, however, saw a major decline in incidences of
embalming, the practice being almost unknown during the nineteenth, before
experiencing a resurrection at the end of the century, in a form which avoided
such gross elements as evisceration, and relied on the use of injected chemicals
to stave off decay.

A feature that has, however, remained a key element of the high-status burial throughout is the leaden coffin. These were originally purely functional boxes, of trapezoidal form. Then from the fifteenth century we frequently find coffins that follow the shape of the body, to produce an effect akin to that of an Egyptian mummy (see p. 99 (fig. 72)). In certain cases, the limbs and even facial features were modelled in the lead, one example being that of Henry, Prince of Wales, son of James VI & I (1612). However, by the later seventeenth century most coffins were of the 'standard' shape, made of flat plates, and tapering towards the head and foot from the elbows; a set of such coffins is to be seen in the vault of Charles II and his successors at Westminster (p. 105 (fig. 77)).

Most leaden cases were enclosed in wooden outer coffins, although most of these had long since come to pieces or disappeared altogether when a number of the royal sepulchres were examined in the nineteenth century. This was partly the result of natural decay, but also of the action of those charged with later burial, who would strip earlier occupants to make room for newcomers; a good example of this is seen in Henry VII's vault at Westminster, when he and his queen lost their wooden cases to make way for James VI & I's interment.

Upholstery was used on the exteriors of many coffins from the seventeenth century onwards, with black or red velvet, together with brass pins, being a common finish. George III, George IV and William IV all had black coffins, contrasting with the scarlet of lesser members of the family. The visceral chests that accompanied coffins were usually of a matching design, although such cases disappear from the record with the decline in the practice of embalming noted above.

As far as the actual tomb is concerned, a wide variety of approaches is seen over the centuries. It always lay in a consecrated place, and for such a distinguished individual as a monarch this would be inside a church. Before to the Reformation, an important imperative was the availability of clergy, monks and nuns to pray for the deceased's soul, with the aim of reducing its stay in Purgatory, the place in which sins were expurgated before the soul passed into Heaven.

Accordingly, many rulers were laid to rest in the churches attached to monasteries. In quite a few cases, a monarch would found a wholly new abbey with the intention of it becoming in due course his place of burial. Such foundations included Ælfred's Winchester New Minster, Henry I's Reading, James I's Perth Charterhouse, Stephen's Faversham and William the Lion's Arbroath. In such establishments, the posthumous welfare of the founder's soul would be a primary care of the abbey personnel.

Some took the alternative approach of adding a chapel to an existing abbey

5. South side of the Confessor's Chapel, Westminster Abbey, showing the table-tombs of Edward III, Princess Margaret (daughter of Edward IV) and Richard II.

church, with dedicated personnel to pray for the founder's soul. Such 'chantries' vary greatly in size and form. Those of Edward IV and Henry V were built high above the tomb itself, overlooking the high altar of the host institution – respectively St George's Chapel at Windsor and Westminster Abbey. Henry VII, in contrast, built a huge structure in place of the old lady chapel at the east end of Westminster Abbey, that would later become the principal burial place of English and British monarchs.

With the ending of Roman Catholic practice under Henry VIII, Edward VI and Elizabeth I, the concept of Purgatory passed from royal burial consideration. Thus, later sepulchres tended to be placed simply within one or other of the established royal burial churches, without major additional architectural provision. As we shall see, however, the nineteenth and twentieth centuries would see faint echoes of ancient tradition of new funerary foundations.

Within the burial church or chapel, for much of mediaeval times the standard form of monument was a 'table-tomb', atop which was placed a stone, metal or wooden effigy of the deceased. This was often equipped with a canopy of some kind, of wood or stone. Perhaps the finest of all is that of Edward II at Gloucester, although some splendid examples exist in Westminster Abbey. Among them are two of the most extravagant, erected by James VI & I for his immediate predecessors – his mother Mary and his cousin Elizabeth I. However, they lie at the end of a chain of evolution: three centuries passed before another monarch would be interred under such a monument.

The earliest of these table-tombs had been themselves sarcophagi, with the king's coffin placed directly inside them. However, by early Lancastrian times the body was being interred in a chamber below the table-tomb itself, which had developed into a proper vault by the reign of Edward IV. Such rooms normally had an entrance that allowed access down a slope or stairway, and although originally intended for one or two burials, larger examples become common during the seventeenth century, used for generations of interments. In some cases, dozens of coffins were piled into a space intended for far fewer. For example, the vault made for Oliver Cromwell in Westminster Abbey was, after his posthumous ejection, used for nineteen coffins, and was later extended to take the total up to fifty-eight.

Such vaults were simply cavities for the storage of coffins, with little thought for their dignified positioning, or access. However, during the eighteenth century far more monumental vaults came into existence, in particular that built by George II below the Henry VII Chapel at Westminster. Here, the monarch and his consort lay in a huge sarcophagus at the end of a passage flanked by rooms containing the remains of their children. George III followed a similar approach under St George's Chapel at Windsor, albeit substituting a podium for the sarcophagus and shelves for side-rooms. This

6. Perhaps the most elaborate monuments erected for British monarchs were the two constructed by James VI & I for his predecessors, Mary of Scotland and Elizabeth I of England. Here, Mary's effigy lies under a great arch, topped by the arms of Scotland.

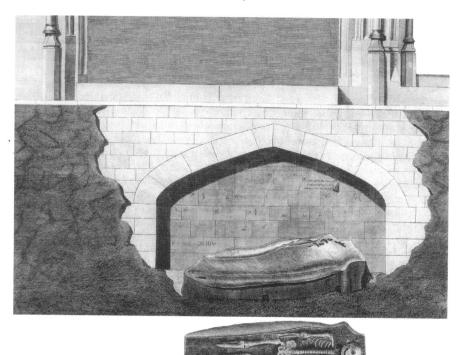

7. Vault of Edward IV, containing the king's lead coffin and his skeleton. The latter retained hair but no flesh, the feet and lower legs being found immersed in fluid in 1788.

vault was intended for generation after generation of royalty, and in their time, George IV and William IV took their places on the podia along the centre of the gothic-vaulted hall.

And then came a complete change. As we have seen, early kings had erected chapels or whole abbeys as their eternal memorials; this custom was essentially revived, on a smaller scale, by Victoria. Inspired by the example of her Saxe-Coburg in-laws and the Orleans royal family of France, she constructed a mausoleum in the grounds of Windsor Castle, in the centre of which was erected another throw-back, a table-tomb not only bearing the effigies of the queen and her husband, but also holding their bodies. Edward VII was buried in a similar tomb; in his case, however, he returned to St George's Chapel, tellingly at the foot of the grave of Henry VI – and directly opposite the sepulchre of the chapel's founder, the fourth Edward.

Edward IV, and Henry V before him, had constructed chantry chapels above their tombs. Five centuries later, a small memorial chapel was added to

8. Four centuries of the English monarchy: the area of the high altar at St George's, Windsor, with the tomb of Henry VI in the centre, and at its foot that of Edward VII. At the lower right is the entrance to the vault containing the bodies of George III, George V and William IV.

the hallowed structure of St George's for George VI, below which he rests with his wife, together with the ashes of their younger daughter. Completed in 1969, this little architectural jewel marks in many ways the timeless nature of Britain's royal tombs, but is yet architecturally very much of its time, one might even say enshrining the continuity and change that has been the key feature of Britain's monarchies over the past fifteen centuries.

I

The Early English Kingdoms

Royal funerary archaeology in the United Kingdom could be regarded as reaching back to the Bronze Age or beyond: the rich barrow burials of the Wessex culture most probably represent the tombs of early chieftains; likewise the passage graves of the Late Neolithic. However, it is not until the seventh century that the sepulchres of credibly kingly individuals appear in the record. The most impressive of these are to be found at Sutton Hoo in Suffolk, and stand at the head of a sequence of royal tombs in England that stretches down to the present day.

As in other parts of this book, only monarchs whose place of burial is known are listed. Intervening rulers are, however, included in the lists on pp. 214-19.

EAST ANGLIA

RÆDWALD (?) (r. c. 599–625)
One of the last pagan kings in England, Rædwald ruled much of England south of the Humber. His prominence and date have long made him the leading candidate for the ownership of Mound 1 at Sutton Hoo, Suffolk, although other names have been mooted.

The tomb
Mound 1 is part of a cemetery used since around the end of the sixth century. As with the adjacent Mound 2 (presumably also a kingly interment), the burial's centrepiece was a massive ship, in the centre of which had been erected a wooden burial chamber. A large quantity of rich funerary equipment was provided, to accompany the body, which lay in a large coffin in the middle of the chamber.

Post-interment history
The cemetery was plundered on a number of occasions, the earliest detectable being dated to the sixteenth century, when large pits were sunk into the top of each mound. Only the contents of Mound 1 escaped the plunderers, whose

9. The great ship in Sutton Hoo mound 1, as seen during the 1939 excavations.

pit penetrated to an insufficient depth. Excavations carried out around 1860 opened Mound 2 and a number of others, but Mound 1 once again escaped. After a long gap, new excavations were begun in 1938 by the then landowner, Edith Pretty. The Mound 1 ship was located in May 1939, excavations subsequently being put under the responsibility of Charles Phillips of Cambridge University. The body had disappeared owing to soil conditions, but could be located by chemical analysis. The wood of the ship had also largely vanished, leaving merely an impression in the soil. The contents of the burial went to the British Museum. The site was re-excavated by the British Museum from 1965 to 1971 under Rupert Bruce-Mitford, with a fresh research campaign initiated at Sutton Hoo in 1983, continuing through the 1990s. This included the excavation of Mound 2 and various other elements of the cemetery.

EDMUND (St) (841–870; r. 855–869)
Apparently of Saxon birth at Nuremberg, but a scion of the East Anglian royal family, Edmund was probably adopted as successor of a King Offa. After the latter's death in the Holy Land, Edmund landed in Norfolk, and was later

elected king and crowned on 25 December 855. His reign was much taken up with resistance to Danish invaders; he was eventually captured and killed by the Viking Hingwar on 20 November 869.

Interment and tomb

Edmund's body, together with its severed head, was recovered and buried at Sutton, near Hellesdon, Norfolk. Here, a chapel was erected over the king's grave, where miracles were soon alleged to have occurred.

Post-interment history

Perhaps around 880, the body was translated to a wooden church at Broedericsworth in Suffolk. Around 927 it was moved to a new shrine, examined and alleged to be incorrupt. It is reported to have been in the same state around 960, by which time it had become a focus for pilgrimage. The body was moved to the church of St Gregory the Great, in St Paul's churchyard, London, in 1009 to protect it from the incursions of Sweyn of Denmark, but was returned to its shrine in 1013.

The body of Edmund was translated in 1032 in the presence of King Cnut to the latter's new abbey at Broedericsworth, which was henceforth known as Bury St Edmunds. It was moved again in 1095, following the building of a new abbey. A fire three years later resulted in the building of a new shrine, the coffin being placed on a stone plinth, covered by a wooden hood, one end of which could be moved to give access. The shrine was destroyed in 1539 at the time of the dissolution of the monasteries, with the probability that the body was then buried near the church.

However, there had since 1450 been a sarcophagus in the Basilica of St Sernin, Toulouse, France, with bones that have been alleged since at least 1580 to be those of Edmund. There is a major problem here, in that there is no evidence for the body of Edmund being removed from Bury at any point after its return from London in 1013. It has been alleged that the remains could have been removed by an agent of Louis in 1217, during his attempt to occupy the English throne (see pp. 61-2). This seems unlikely, both on circumstantial grounds and because the period of his campaign is well recorded in contemporary sources, and there is no hint of such a desecration in them.

The bones alleged to be Edmund's – a complete skeleton – were moved in 1644 to a pair of silver reliquaries in the Toulouse basilica. During the French Revolution, the reliquaries were taken away, but the bones left. The skull was removed for safety in July 1795, but the skeleton remained in situ. The former was returned to the basilica in 1802, and placed in a reliquary of bronze in 1845.

At the end of the nineteenth century, Cardinal Herbert Alfred Vaughan (1832–1903) managed to obtain the skeleton for installation in Westminster Cathedral. The bones arrived at Newhaven on 25 July 1901, and were placed in the chapel of the Duke of Norfolk at Arundel Castle, pending the completion of the cathedral. However, doubts as to whether they truly are those of Edmund mean that the bones remain at Arundel to this day.

ESSEX

SAEBERHT (r. *c.* 603–616)
The first Christian king of Essex.

Tomb and interment
Saeberht was the traditional founder of Westminster Abbey, and is said to have been buried there. However, a wooden burial chamber (4 metres square by 1.5 metres high) under a small barrow at Prittlewell, Southend, Essex, appears to be from the early seventh century, with grave goods in pagan style, but also a pair of gold crosses on the body. Such a combination would fit the

10. Alleged tomb of Saeberht at Westminster Abbey.

context of the convert Saeberht, or one of his immediate successors, perhaps Sigeberht I (d. 653).

Material placed in the tomb included a sword and shield, a folding stool, a hanging bowl adorned with metal strips and medallions, two cauldrons, four coloured glass vessels, a gold reliquary, a flagon, eight wooden drinking cups decorated with gilded mounts, two drinking horns, a lyre, and several iron-clad barrels and buckets, together with a large casket, perhaps for textiles. Much of this material seems to have been of overseas origin, as certainly were a pair of gold coins from Merovingian France.

Post-interment history

The Westminster remains believed to be Saeberht's were moved to the south side of the entrance to the chapter house under Henry III, and then shifted to a Purbeck marble sarcophagus in the quire, south of the altar, in 1307. At this translation the right arm was still clothed with skin.

The Southend tomb was found on a verge between a road and a railway line in 2003 during a pre-road improvement survey by consultants Atkins Heritage and the Museum of London Archaeology Service working for Southend-on-Sea Borough Council. The roof of the tomb had collapsed but the contents were untouched; however, the body had been destroyed by the acidity of the soil.

SEBBI (d. *c.* 695; r. 664–*c.* 694)

This king reigned jointly with his nephew, Sighere; he abdicated to become a monk shortly before his death. He was buried in St Paul's Cathedral, London; a tomb called his lay adjacent to that of Æthelred II of England in the seventeenth century.

KENT

ÆTHELBERT I (r. 560–616)

The son of his predecessor, Eomenric, and the first Christian king in England, Æthelbert was buried at Canterbury in the abbey founded by Augustine, in the Porticus of St Martin, on the south side of the Church of SS Peter and Paul. His body was subsequently reburied above the high altar when the abbey was rebuilt and was lost during the dissolution of the monasteries.

EADBALD (r. 616–640)
EARCONBERT (r. 640–664)
ECGBRIHT I (r. 664–673)
HLOTHERE (r. 673–685)
WIHTRED (r. 690–725)

All these monarchs were interred in the church of St Mary in St Augustine's Abbey. Their remains were temporarily moved to the western tower when the church was demolished, and then reburied in the south transept in the late 1080s; their location is marked by modern tombs.

ÆTHELBERT II (r. 725–762)

A son of Wihtred, Æthelbert was buried in St Mary's Abbey at Reculver, Kent, built in 699. The church was extensively rebuilt during the twelfth and thirteenth centuries and demolished in 1809. However, its twelfth-century twin towers (whose spires were removed in 1880) were left standing as a navigational aid to shipping. The king's tomb was allegedly still locatable in the south aisle in the seventeenth century.

MERCIA

WULFHERE (r. 657–674)

The son of Penda of Mercia, Wulfhere returned from exile after two years of Northumbrian rule over his realm. He became the first Christian king of Mercia and greatly enlarged her dominions, even invading the Isle of Wight. Wulfhere was buried at Lichfield.

ÆTHELRED (r. 674–704)

A son of Penda, Æthelred abdicated to become a monk at Bardney, Lincolnshire, where he eventually became Abbot. Presumably owing to his presence in the area, a grassy mound nearby became known as the 'King's Grave'.

COENRED (r. 704–709)

A son of Wulfhere, Coenred abdicated the throne to become a monk at Rome, where he was buried in the Church of St Mary in the English College.

CEOLRED (r. 709–716)

A son of Æthelred, the brother and successor of Wulfhere, Ceolred unsuccessfully invaded Wessex in 715, and died insane the following year. He was buried at Lichfield.

ÆTHELBALD (r. 716–757)
The grandson of Eowa, brother of Penda, the king's conquests led to him styling himself 'King of Britain'. He was, however, ultimately murdered by his own household five years later at Seckington, Staffordshire.

Interment and tomb
Æthelbald was interred in the Church of St Wystan, Repton, in a crypt built around 750.

Post-interment history
A lead coffin was found during the digging of a tunnel from the crypt into the church in 1792; it bore, in Latin, the inscription 'imperial soul in narrow place', which could suggest royal ownership. It was reburied a metre below the pavement, to the left of the tunnel, but no details are recorded of its form.

OFFA (r. 757–796)
A descendant of Eowa, brother and successor of Penda, Offa ultimately ruled much of southern and central England, claiming the title of 'King of the English'. The builder of the eponymous dyke to mark the western boundary of his kingdom, Offa corresponded with Charlemagne and was a patron of religious houses.

Interment and tomb
Offa was buried in a chapel on the bank of the River Ouse at Bedford. This was lost when erosion of the bank led to the building's collapse into the river.

EGFRITH (r. 787–796)
Offa's son, Egfrith served as his father's co-regent, but survived him by only five months. He was buried at St Albans, Hertfordshire, in an abbey church founded by Offa.

COENWULF (r. 796–821)
A descendant of Penda's father, Coenwulf died in Basingwerk just before a campaign against the Welsh. He was buried in Winchcombe Abbey.

Post-interment history
Winchcombe Abbey was destroyed during the dissolution of the monasteries. Around 1815 a pair of early stone coffins were found within the eastern wall of the church, beneath the location of the high altar, one that of an adult and one that of a child. The former, containing a skeleton that fell to dust, was

11. Crypt of St Wystan's Church, Repton, possibly built for the burial of Æthelbald.

12. The entrance to the crypt of St Wystan's now lies at the east end of the north aisle of the church (marked by bright spot of light).

attributed to Coenwulf, the latter to his son, Cenelm (q.v.). The coffins were sold to the proprietor of Warmington Grange, where they were displayed.

CENELM (St) (r. 821)

Coenwulf's son was chosen to succeed him, but was soon killed. It remains a matter of debate whether he was an adult slain in battle or a child murdered by a jealous sister, as legend would have it. In any case, he was later canonised. He was buried at Winchcombe Abbey, and if really a child might have been buried in a stone coffin found around 1815 (see previous entry).

WIGLAF (r. 827–829 & 830–840)

The successor of Ludecan, Wiglaf was driven from his throne by Egbert of Wessex, and then restored as the latter's vassal. He was buried in St Wystan's, Repton, in a 'mausoleum' – presumably the crypt. He was later joined there by his grandson, St Wystan, murdered in 849. See p. 23 above for the discovery of a potential royal coffin in 1792.

BURHED (d. 874/5; r. 852–874)

This king lost his throne to the Danes and went to Rome, where he died and was buried in the Church of St Mary in the English College.

NORTHUMBRIA

EDWIN (*c.* 585–633; r. 616–633)
Son of Ælla, King of Deira, who had been deposed in 588, Edwin returned from exile and united Northumbria, also converting to Christianity. He was killed in battle with Penda of Mercia. Edwin's body was buried at Whitby, his head at York.

OSWALD (St) (*c.* 605–642; r. 634–642)
The son of King Æthelfrith, Oswald restored Christianity and built up an empire that covered much of Britain. He was, however, killed by Penda of Mercia near Huddersfield.

Tomb and interment
Oswald's body was hacked to pieces and his head and arms stuck on poles; parts of the body were subsequently claimed by various monasteries. The remains of the body were subsequently buried at Bardney Abbey, Lincolnshire, by the king's niece, Queen Osthryth of Mercia. The head and hands were taken to Bamborough, and the head then to Lindisfarne, founded by Oswald's friend, St Aidan.

Post-interment history
Bardney Abbey was subsequently destroyed by the Vikings; however, the saintly remains there were translated to St Oswald's Priory Church, Gloucester, in 909. Around 1113, some relics were moved within the church, although a contemporary account states that they now comprised a left arm and hair, rather than the 'body' that earlier ones ascribe to Gloucester. All trace of them is now lost.

The remains of the skull went with the body of St Cuthbert from Lindisfarne to Durham Cathedral in 1104. The shrines of the saints were destroyed in 1537, and their bones finally buried together in St Cuthbert's grave in 1542. The tomb was opened in 1827, the saints' bones being again examined and provided with a definitive new coffin, in 1899. Four fragments of the brain-case of Oswald's skull survived, showing clear signs of having been split with a heavy, sharp weapon – indeed, it appears that the back of the skull had been shorn off. A lower jaw also seems to have been that of the king, as may have been one or more ribs.

OSWINE (St) (r. 644–651)
King of Deira, the portion of Northumbria between the Tees and the Humber,

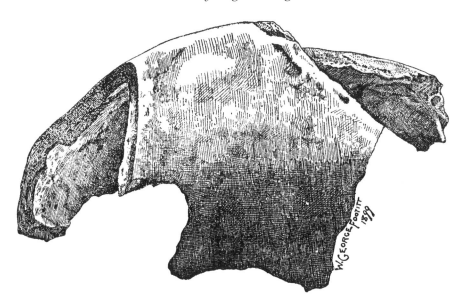

13. Fragments of the skull of St Oswald.

and son of its king, Osric, Oswine was murdered at the instigation of Oswiu of Bernicia, the northern part of Northumbria.

Tomb and interment
The king was buried in the churchyard of St Mary at Tynemouth, where a shrine grew up. The grave was later lost, but re-found in 1065, when the remains were translated to a new resting place. They were finally lost at the dissolution of the monasteries.

OSWIU (*c.* 612–670; r. 642–670)
The son of Æthelfrith of Bernicia, and brother of Oswald, Oswiu finally united Northumbria, spending much of his reign engaged in warfare. He was buried at Whitby.

ECGFRITH (r. 670–685)
A son of Oswiu, Ecgfrith was killed at the Battle of Dunnichen, and buried on Iona.

ALDFRITH (r. 685–705)
The (probably) illegitimate son of Oswiu, Aldfrith succeeded his brother Ecgfrith. The king died at Driffield, although whether from illness or wounds, received in battle at Ebberston, near Scarborough, remains uncertain.

Interment and tomb

Aldfrith was buried in St Mary's (called St Peter's in eighteenth/nineteenth centuries) Church at Little Driffield, Yorkshire.

Post-interment history

In later years, Aldfrith became confounded in some minds with Alfred of Wessex. In 1784, the Society of Antiquaries sponsored a search for the body of the king; it was claimed that a skeleton and fragments of armour were found in a stone coffin in the chancel, but this was later denied by the then curate. In 1807, when the church was being rebuilt, a further investigation was made and it was found that the church and the chancel were now smaller than had been originally the case, suggesting that the king's burial might now lie outside.

A tablet recording the king's interment lies on the south side of the chancel, the text of which was formerly painted on the north wall. The text's origin is not known but had been renewed (and revised) at least twice before the early nineteenth century.

CEOLWULF (St) (d. 764; r. 729–737)

The brother of his predecessor, Coenred, Ceolwulf was deposed, forced to become a monk, and then restored in 731. However, six years later he abdicated and became a monk at Lindisfarne, where he was buried near St Cuthbert.

Post-interment history

In 830 Ceolwulf's remains were translated to the porch of the new Church of St Cuthbert at Norham-on-Tweed, which probably lay to the east of the present building (begun in 1165). Ceolwulf's head was later transferred to Durham Cathedral, but was lost at the Reformation, not being among the relics found in St Cuthbert's grave in 1899.

EADBERHT (d. 768; r. 737–758)

The cousin of Ceolwulf, Eadberht emulated him in becoming a monk, following a crushing military defeat. As a monk at St Peter's, York, he was buried there.

ÆLFWALD I (r. 779–789)

The son of his predecessor, Oswulf, Ælfwald was assassinated, probably at Chesters, at the instigation of the noble Sicga. He was buried at Hexham Abbey, under a slab adorned with vines and fruit.

OSRED II (d. 792; r. 788–790)

The son of a deposed predecessor, Osred was captured by Æthelred I, who had previously ruled Northumbria in 774–778/9, deposed and exiled to a monastery on the Isle of Man. He later attempted to regain his throne, but was deserted by his supporters and killed at Aynburg. His remains were buried at Tynemouth Priory.

OSBALD (d. 799; r. 796)

This king reigned for twenty-seven days, before being outlawed and exiled to Lindisfarne. He later left and became an Abbot among the Picts, and was buried in York.

WESSEX

CYNEGILS (r. 611–643)

Probably the son of Ceol, Cynegils, together with his son, was responsible for a victory over the Britons at Beandûn in 614, but was defeated by Edwin of Northumbria in 626. He was baptised in 635.

Interment and tomb

Cynegils' body was buried before the high altar in the then incomplete Old Minster at Winchester, which he had begun.

Post-interment history

The remains were moved to Winchester Cathedral at some point after the demolition of the Old Minster in 1093, and certainly by 1158. Bones identified as his were placed with others attributed to Æthelwulf in a mortuary chest near the shrine of St Swithun; they now lie on top of a screen of the presbytery. For their various moves, see pp. 196-201. The fifteenth-century inner mortuary chest of Cynegils and Æthelwulf is now displayed in the cathedral's Triforium Gallery.

CENEWALH (r. 643–645 & 648–674)

Cenewalh was the son of Cynegils, but was soon driven from his throne by Penda of Mercia. He converted to Christianity in East Anglian exile, and after his restoration completed the Old Minster at Winchester.

Interment and tomb

Cenewalh was buried before (or under) the high altar at Winchester in 674; nothing is known of the later fate of his remains.

SEAXBURH (r. 672–674)

The widow of Cenewalh, Seaxburh ruled alone after his death. It is assumed that she was buried at Winchester.

ÆSCWINE (r. 674–676)

A great-great-grandson of Ceolwulf, Æscwine was buried in the Old Minster at Winchester.

Post-interment history

Æscwine's bones were among those moved to Winchester Cathedral in 1158, grouped with those of Centwine, but his name no longer features in the inscriptions of any of the mortuary chests there.

CENTWINE (r. 676–685)

A son of Cynegils, Centwine added the Quantocks to Wessex, but was deposed by Cædwalla. He was buried at Winchester.

Post-interment history

Centwine's bones were among those moved to Winchester Cathedral in 1158, grouped with those of Æscwine, but his name no longer features in the inscriptions of any of the mortuary chests there.

CÆDWALLA (*c.* 659–689; r. 685–688)

This king was a usurper, having previously attempted to seize Sussex, killing its king, Æthelwealh. He then later attacked Kent and the Isle of Wight, before abdicating and retiring to Rome where he was baptised by Pope Sergius I, dying ten days later and being interred at St Peter's, Rome. His epitaph was allegedly found in the fifteenth century, but is now lost.

INA (d. 728; r. 688–726)

Elected king, Ina extended the power of Wessex still further. He retired to Rome as a monk, founding a hospice for English pilgrims in Rome.

Interment and tomb

Ina was buried in the Church of San-Spirito-in-Sassia in the district of Borgo in Rome.

ÆTHELHEARD (r. 726–741)

The king was buried at Winchester, but nothing is known of the details.

14. Fifteenth-century mortuary chest of Cynewulf and Egbert, Winchester Cathedral.

CUTHRED (r. 741–754)
A relative of Æthelheard, Cuthred was buried at Winchester, but nothing is known of the details.

SIGEBERHT (r. 754–757)
This king was deposed, but briefly retained Hampshire before being killed. He was apparently buried at Winchester.

CYNEWULF (r. 757–786)
This monarch fought against the Welsh, but was assassinated by Cyneheard, son of the King Sigeberht whom Cynewulf had previously dethroned.

Interment and tomb
Cynewulf was buried in the Old Minster at Winchester.

Post-interment history
Cynewulf's remains were moved to Winchester Cathedral between the demolition of the Old Minster in 1093 and 1158. For their various moves, see pp. 196-201.

BEORHRIC (r. 786–802)
Married to Eadburh, daughter of Offa of Mercia, Beorhric died from poison prepared by her. He was buried at Wareham.

EGBERT (*c.* 775–839; r. 802–839)
The son of Ealhmund, under-king of Kent (d. 786), Egbert was a descendant of Ina's brother, and after living at the court of Charlemagne obtained the throne of Wessex. His power was then extended over Kent and Northumbria.

Interment and tomb
Egbert was buried in the Old Minster at Winchester.

Post-interment history
Egbert's remains were moved to Winchester Cathedral after the demolition of the Old Minster in 1093, and certainly by 1158. Bones identified as his were placed with others attributed to Cynewulf in a mortuary chest; for their various moves, see above and pp. 196-201.

ÆTHELWULF (*c*. 800–858; r. 839–855)
A son of Egbert, Æthelwulf was made king of Kent, Sussex and Surrey by his father in 828, and also served as Bishop of Winchester. He made a pilgrimage to Rome and was also successful in battle against the Danes. He gave up the Wessex throne to his rebellious son, Æthelbald, but remained under-king of Kent.

Interment and tomb
The king was buried in the Old Minster at Winchester.

Post-interment history
His remains were moved to Winchester Cathedral after the demolition of the Old Minster in 1093, and certainly by 1158. His alleged bones were placed with those attributed to Cynegils. For their various moves, see pp. 196-201.

15. Fifteenth-century mortuary chest of Cynegils and Æthelwulf, Winchester Cathedral.

16. Mortuary chest bearing the names of Cynegils and Æthelwulf, Winchester Cathedral.

ÆTHELBALD (*c.* 834–860; r. 855–860)

The second son of Æthelwulf, Æthelbald displaced his father from the Wessex throne and married his stepmother.

Interment and tomb

Buried in Sherborne Abbey behind the high altar.

Post-interment history

In November 1801, while digging burial vaults at the east end of the north aisle of the quire, a stone coffin was found; the skull within crumbled on being touched. This may have been the burial of either Æthelbald or Æthelbert. The coffin is now on display in this location, together with a brass plaque. Another similar coffin, containing bones, is visible under a glass sheet immediately to the north.

ÆTHELBERT (c. 836–866; r. 860–866)

A younger brother of his predecessor, who now held both the throne of Wessex and the various under-kingships, Æthelbert's reign was marred by Danish attacks.

Interment and tomb
Buried in Sherborne Abbey behind the high altar.

Post-interment history
See Æthelbald.

ÆTHELRED I (d. 871; r. 866–871)

A brother of his two predecessors, Æthelred spent much of his reign fighting the Danes in both Mercia and Wessex. Ultimately, however, he was mortally wounded in a battle at Martin, near Cranborne.

Interment and tomb
The king was buried at Wimborne Minster.

Post-interment history
The church has been rebuilt on a number of occasions. A fourteenth/fifteenth-century brass of Æthelred is affixed to the wall north of the high altar, with a copper inscription of around the seventeenth century.

17. High altar of Wimborne Minster; the brass of Æthelred I is on the left. Opposite is the tomb of John Beaufort, Duke of Somerset (1373-1410) and his Duchess, Margaret Holland (later Duchess of Clarence, daughter-in-law of Henry IV), parents of Lady Margaret Beaufort.

18. Brass of Æthelred I.

ÆLFRED (849–899; r. 871–899)

The son of Æthelwulf, he was the fourth and last of the brothers to take the throne. Much of his reign was spent in battle against the Danes, but he also did much to promote learning in the consolidation of Wessex as the basis for the later English kingdom.

Interment and tomb

The king was provisionally buried in the Winchester Old Minster, but translated to the New Minster, a building begun just before Ælfred's death, soon after its dedication in 903. The body was buried in front of the high altar.

Post-interment history

The body was moved once again in 1112 to Hyde Abbey on the demolition of the New Minster; the former was demolished at the Reformation. The site was cleared of rubble in 1788 during the building of a new gaol. During the digging of pits to bury the larger material, the prisoners uncovered the site of the high altar and three graves – apparently those of Ælfred, his wife, and Edward the Elder. A reported stone coffin encased in lead has been identified as Ælfred's: the lead was sold, the bones scattered and the remains of the coffin deeply buried, below the water-table.

19. Excavation of the eastern end of Hyde Abbey, showing the location of the royal tombs before the former high altar, in front of the light-coloured cars on the right.

John Mellor, described by the local vicar at the time as 'a rogue and a charlatan' dug a pit in the same area in the mid-1860s, finding bones he claimed to have been Ælfred's. Having allegedly been exhibited for a time, they were ultimately buried under a slab, marked with a simple cross, outside the east end of the Church of St Bartholomew nearby. A further trench was dug by Alfred Bowker, Mayor of Winchester, in 1897. The area was excavated by the Winchester Museums Service in 1999, identifying the probable remains of the grave-cuts, but no trace of their contents.

EDWARD 'THE ELDER' (869–924; r. 899–924)
The son of Ælfred, Edward defeated and killed his cousin and rival for the throne, Æthelwald, a son of Æthelred I, in 905. He greatly extended the power of Wessex, annexing Mercia and receiving the submission of the Danes of East Anglia and Essex. He died at Farndon-on-Dee.

Interment and tomb
Edward was interred alongside his parents in front of the high altar in the Winchester New Minster.

Post-interment history
The king's bones were moved to Hyde in 1112 and suffered the same fate as those of his father, being scattered in 1788.

ÆTHELSTAN (895–940; r. 924–939)
The son of Edward the Elder, Æthelstan made conquests that presaged the permanent union of all of England under Edgar.

Interment and tomb
The king was buried under the high altar at Malmesbury Abbey.

Post-interment history
The tomb was opened around 1130/40 and the body found to be in good condition. A later monument of a kingly figure was in the south-east corner of the church, some way from the king's likely burial place, until 1928, when it was moved to the west end of the north aisle during restoration work. The face of the effigy has been replaced.

EDMUND I (921–946; r. 939–946)
A half-brother of his predecessor, Edmund continued the wars of unification,

20. The tomb known as that of Æthelstan at Malmesbury.

21. Mortuary chest bearing the name 'Edmund' in Winchester Cathedral.

22. View of the presbytery at Glastonbury. The modern sign in the middle distance and the slab beyond mark the location of the tomb of 'Arthur': by the sixteenth century it was flanked by the tombs of Edmund I and II.

but was stabbed and killed by a robber named Liofa at Pucklechurch, South Gloucestershire.

Interment and tomb

The king was buried at Glastonbury Abbey, in the northern part of the tower.

Post-interment history

By the sixteenth century the body lay in the presbytery, on one side of the supposed reburial of King Arthur. The alleged bones of the latter and Queen Guinevere had been found in 1191 and placed in a tomb in the presbytery on 19 April 1278. The tombs of both 'Arthur' and Edmund were destroyed at the time of the dissolution of the monasteries.

EADRED (r. 946–955)

Edmund I's younger brother Eadred's reign featured conflicts with Wulfstan, Archbishop of York, and with Eric Bloodaxe of Northumbria.

Interment and tomb

Eadred was buried in the Old Minster at Winchester.

Post-interment history

The remains were moved to Winchester Cathedral between 1093 and 1158; for their various moves, see pp. 196-201.

EDWY (*c.* 941–959; r. 955–959)

The eldest son of Edmund I, Edwy was forced to cede the northern part of his dominions to his brother, Edgar. He died at Gloucester in suspicious circumstances.

Interment and tomb

Edwy was buried at Winchester, but nothing is known about the later fate of his bones.

II

England

HOUSE OF WESSEX

EDGAR (944–975; r. 959–975)
The younger brother of Edwy, Edgar had been given the rule of the northern portion of the Wessex domains in 957. Having consolidated his power, he was crowned the first King of the English at Bath in 973.

Interment and tomb
Edgar was buried at Glastonbury.

Post-interment history
The body was moved within the abbey by Abbot Æthelweard in 1052. It was allegedly found in good condition, and is said to have bled profusely when dismembered to allow it to fit in the reliquary which had been prepared for the royal remains – the abbot consequently going insane and falling to his death. The king's new shrine lay near the high altar, but was lost with the destruction of the abbey.

EDWARD 'THE MARTYR' (963–978; r. 975–978)
Edward was Edgar's son by his first wife. His election was not unopposed and he was murdered at Corfe Castle, Dorset, at the instigation of his step-mother, Ælfryth.

Interment and tomb
Placed in a hut after his murder, the king was buried on 13 February 979 at the east end of the church of St Mary in Wareham.

Post-interment history
On 18 February 980, Edward's body was moved to the abbey church of St Mary and St Edward at Shaftesbury. He was originally buried on the north side of the principal altar, but subsequently, on 20 June 1001, translated to a position in the sanctuary at the east end, joining other relics there. Some bones

23. Ruins of Shaftesbury Abbey from the south-east; the finding place of the alleged bones of Edward the Martyr lies beyond the modern altar, in front of the stone shrine built to receive them in the 1930s.

were transferred to Abingdon Abbey in 1034, while other relics were held at Leominster, Salisbury, Bradford-on-Avon and Winchester.

Shaftesbury church is now reduced to its foundations. The first excavations took place in 1816; a grave on the north side of the high altar was regarded as possibly that of the king, but when it was opened in 1861 it was found to be empty, with the exception of the remains of an iron-bound box and a metatarsal bone. In 1902/4, a glass bowl was found in front of the high altar under a heart-shaped white marble slab. It is possible that this was a reliquary, as it is known that part of a lung of the king was preserved for some time.

On 24 January 1931, a leaden casket was found during an excavation in the ruins by their owner's son, John Wilson Claridge (1905–1993). The casket (60 x 23 centimetres) lay in the north-east corner of the north transept under a stone slab and contained an incomplete skeleton. The bones were soon afterwards subject to an examination by Dr T.E.A. Stowell, who believed that their context, maturity and the injuries displayed strongly suggested that they were those of the king. A later investigation by Dr Don Brothwell in 1973/4 cast doubt on the age at death of the remains, suggesting that the individual was too old to be Edward. Nevertheless, a Carbon-14 determination in 1988 gave a 95% probability that the bones dated to 680–1030, and a 68% one that their owner had died between 810 and 980.

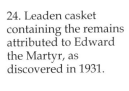

24. Leaden casket containing the remains attributed to Edward the Martyr, as discovered in 1931.

Claridge erected a shrine adjacent to the bones' place of discovery, in which they remained until the abbey site was sold in 1951. Claridge moved to Malta in 1970, the bones remaining behind in the vault of the Midland Bank at Woking. Following several approaches to organisations who might enshrine the bones and make them 'available for prayer and reverence', the Russian Orthodox Church in Exile offered to take them, and acquired a former chapel in Brookwood Cemetery, Surrey, to house them.

An enshrinement ceremony was held in September 1984 – but without the bones, which were now the subject of a dispute between Claridge and his elder brother, Geoffrey, who wanted them to return to Shaftesbury. Although the case was dismissed, concerns as to the security of the Brookwood chapel, and further legal action by Geoffrey's daughter, meant that the actual enshrinement of the bones at Brookwood did not occur until December 1988, legal action continuing until 1995.

When a new altar was erected at Shaftesbury in that same year it incorporated a cavity against the possibility that the bones might one day return to the abbey ruins.

ÆTHELRED II 'THE UNREADY' (968–1016; r. 978–1013 & 1014–1016)

The half-brother of his murdered predecessor, Æthelred had a turbulent reign, including a Scots invasion and continual conflict with the Danes. He was driven into exile in 1013, but was restored the following year.

Interment and tomb
The king was buried in St Paul's Cathedral, London.

Post-interment history
By the seventeenth century the body lay in a massive grey coffin, with semi-circular arcading and supported on four legs, at the western end of the north quire aisle. The burial was broken open during the Commonwealth and finally lost with the destruction of the old St Paul's in the Great Fire of London.

HOUSE OF DENMARK

SWEYN (d. 1014; r. 1013–1014)
Æthelred was driven from his throne by Sweyn, who had ruled the Danes intermittently since 986. Sweyn's death at Gainsborough, seven months after being acknowledged as 'full king' was ascribed to the vengeance of St Edmund of East Anglia for threatening Bury St Edmunds with destruction.

Interment and tomb
Sweyn was initially buried in a large tumulus on the edge of Thonock Park, at Castle Hills, Cambridgeshire. The body was later embalmed and taken back to Denmark for interment in the Hellig Trefoldig, Roskilde Cathedral.

HOUSE OF WESSEX

EDMUND II 'IRONSIDE' (989–1016; r. 1016)
Succeeding his father, Æthelred II, Edmund initially defeated Cnut, but was forced to cede the North of England to Cnut, dying suddenly soon afterwards.

Interment and tomb
The king was buried at Glastonbury. One of the mortuary chests in

Winchester Cathedral is inscribed for an 'Edmund', but is almost certainly the eldest son of Ælfred.

Post-interment history
By the sixteenth century placed opposite that of Edmund I, flanking 'Arthur', the king's tomb was lost at the dissolution of the monasteries.

HOUSE OF DENMARK

CNUT (c. 995–1035; r. 1016–1035)
Cnut, who had succeeded his father Sweyn as king of Denmark in 1014, was chosen as English king by the Witan (traditional assembly). He made many religious endowments, and visited Rome in 1027.

Interment and tomb
Cnut was buried in the Old Minster at Winchester, either near the high altar or adjacent to the shrine erected above the former grave of St Swithun.

Post-interment history
The remains were moved to Winchester Cathedral after the demolition of the Old Minster in 1093, and certainly by 1158. His bones were placed in a mortuary chest near the shrine of St Swithun; in 1460 their coffer was located above the door to the 'south crypt' of the cathedral. Cnut's remains now lie in chests on top of one or more screens of the presbytery. For their various moves, see pp. 196-201. An alleged discovery of his corpse in 1766 by workmen seems to have been based on the re-use of a slab naming him in a far later interment.

HAROLD I 'HAREFOOT' (1016/17–1040; r. 1035–1040)
A son of Cnut, Harold engineered his election as king of northern England, and then all of England (1037).

Interment and tomb
The king was initially buried at Westminster.

Post-interment history
The remains were disinterred by Harthacnut, decapitated and thrown in water, but were retrieved and ultimately buried at St Clement Danes, Strand, London.

25. Northern mortuary chest at Winchester, bearing the names of Cnut, William II, Emma, Wina and Ælfwine.

26. Tomb of Harthacnut, Winchester Cathedral.

HARTHACNUT (*c.* 1018–1042; r. 1040–1042)

Succeeding Cnut in Denmark in 1035 and finally elected king of England on Harold I's death, Harthacnut died suddenly at a feast.

Interment and tomb

The king was buried in the Old Minster at Winchester.

Post-interment history

Harthacnut's remains were moved to Winchester Cathedral between 1093 and 1158. His bones were placed in a mortuary chest near the shrine of St Swithun, at one point possibly together with those of Cnut. However, they were ultimately interred below the eastern arch on the north side of the presbytery. The tomb was remodelled and given plaques facing the north aisle in 1525.

HOUSE OF WESSEX

EDWARD 'THE CONFESSOR' (1002–1066; r. 1042–1066)

A son of Æthelred II and the half-brother of Harthacnut, Edward was a great patron of the church, rebuilding Westminster Abbey. His in-laws, the Godwins, dominated the affairs of the country.

Interment and tomb

Edward was buried in his new abbey, before the high altar.

Post-interment history

The king's grave was opened by Henry I, and then under Henry II when Edward was canonised in 1163. On the latter occasion the body is alleged to have been perfectly preserved; his ring and vestments were on this occasion removed, the latter to make three copes. At the rebuilding of Westminster Abbey by Henry III, the sainted king's body was installed in a shrine, comprising a wooden superstructure above an arcaded stone base. In a cavity in the top of the latter was placed the coffin. Edward's old coffin was later used for the initial interment of Henry III (q.v.).

At the time of the dissolution of the monasteries the coffin was removed, apparently by dismantling the stones at one end of the shrine, and buried nearby. The whole shrine was then taken down, but was reassembled under Mary I, and formally reinstated on 20 March 1557, a painted inscription also being added naming the king. However, it seems to have been rebuilt in a hurry and parts placed erroneously, with the number of steps at the base reduced from four. Also, the altar that had apparently lain at the western end

27. Reconstruction of the shrine of Edward the Confessor, Westminster Abbey, with the superstructure raised to reveal the saint's casket.

may have been re-employed to rebury some children of Henry III and Edward I, just west of the entrance to the Chapel of St Edmund.

Although the body was allegedly incorrupt in 1163, decay had occurred by 1685, when a hole 'appeared' in the coffin lid, and parts of what was now a skeleton were examined. The head was 'sound and firm, with upper and nether Jaws whole and full of Teeth, with a lift of Gold above an Inch broad in the nature of a Coronet, surrounding the Temples: There was also in the Coffin white-Linnen, and Gold-colour'd flowr'd-silk, that look't indifferent fresh. ... There were all his Bones, and much dust likewise' (Taylour 1685). Following this examination, a new outer coffin was made, 225 x 66/58.5 x 58.5 centimetres, probably to fit the original case.

The tomb was examined once more in 1916 following the temporary removal of the wooden superstructure as part of civil defence preparations in the abbey.

HOUSE OF GODWIN

HAROLD II (*c.* 1022–1066; r. 1066)
The brother-in-law of Edward the Confessor, Harold repulsed a Danish invasion in September 1066, but was killed the following month at the Battle of Hastings by William of Normandy – afterwards William I.

Interment and tomb
Accounts of the fate of Harold's body are inconsistent. William rejected an offer by Harold's mother, Gytha, to buy the body for its weight in gold, and according to the Norman chronicler, William of Jumieges, it was buried on the sea shore.

Tradition generally holds that the body was subsequently taken to Waltham (Holy Cross) Abbey and reburied in front of its high altar, and in 1120 moved to the nave. A fourteenth-century account records that it by then had a image of the king. When the abbey was dissolved in Henry VIII's time the church was considerably reduced in size and the nave demolished. The assumed site of Harold's body now lies in the church grounds.

However, an incomplete skeleton found in 1954 in Bosham church, Harold's family church, has been claimed to be that of the king, on the grounds that the unhealed fracture of its left femur reflected injuries inflicted on his body at Hastings. During 2003 an application was made to reopen the grave to extract DNA samples; this was rejected by the diocesan advisory committee, a ruling upheld on appeal by a consistory court in December 2003. In any case, other members of the Godwin family are also known to have been buried there, and no definitive evidence exists as to the true place of interment of Harold's corpse.

HOUSE OF NORMANDY

WILLIAM I (1028–1087; r. 1066–1087)

As Duke of Normandy, William had at one point been promised the throne by Edward the Confessor, and invaded in 1066 on Harold II's accession. In 1087 he suffered an internal rupture caused by a riding accident while besieging Mantes in France, and died six weeks later.

Interment and tomb

The king was interred in St Stephen's Abbey, Caen, Normandy. It was reported that the body was forced into too short a stone coffin and ruptured, leading to an awful smell pervading the church. The monument, commissioned by William II, was executed by Otto the Goldsmith, 'resplendent with gold, silver and gems'; a recumbent effigy was added later. It lay in the middle of the quire, just before the high altar.

Post-interment history

The king's tomb was opened in 1522 at the behest of an Italian cardinal; the body was reported to be well preserved, appearing tall and corpulent. A picture was painted of the body, which was hung on the wall of the church, opposite the monument, which was carefully closed. However, on 8/9 May 1562 the church was pillaged by a Huguenot mob; the tomb was opened and found to contain bones 'wrapped in taffeta'. These were flung around the church, and although an attempt was made to gather them up, the monks were driven away and the bones further scattered. Only a thighbone could be recovered and was ultimately returned to the abbey in 1642 by the Vicomte de Falaise, enclosed in a lead casket.

For the reburial, a table tomb was erected in the centre of the quire. The sides were of speckled marble, with at the head and the foot respectively the heraldic symbols of England and of Normandy. In 1742, this monument was removed and the bone placed under an inscribed floor slab in the sanctuary. This was smashed during the French Revolution, being replaced by a more elaborate one in 1802 at the direction of General Dugua, Prefect of Calvados.

WILLIAM II (*c.* 1057–1100; r. 1087–1100)

The second son of William I, the king was known as 'Rufus' on account of his red hair. He died in the New Forest from an arrow-shot while hunting. It remains uncertain whether or not this was an accident.

28. Tomb of William I in front of the high altar of his abbey at Caen.

29. Southern of the two Winchester mortuary chests bearing the names of Cnut, William II, Emma, Wina and Ælfwine.

Interment and tomb

William was buried in Winchester Cathedral, under the tower: his presence was believed to be the cause of the latter's collapse in 1107. According to John Stow (1592) the burial was 'under a playne flat marble stone, before the lecturne in the queere' – apparently also signifying the place below the tower. Another tomb long identified as the king's is now regarded as that of a mediaeval bishop, probably Henry of Blois (d. 1171: brother of King Stephen).

Post-interment history

Also according to Stow, by 1592 the king's bones had 'long since' been transferred into a mortuary chest alongside those of Cnut. They had probably been moved around 1525, when all the other royal bodies in the cathedral were rearranged. They now lie mixed with others atop one or more screens of the presbytery. For their various moves, see pp. 200-1.

HENRY I (1068–1135; r. 1100–1135)

The youngest son of William I, Henry was elected king by the Witan, ignoring the claims of his elder brother Robert, Duke of Normandy. A vigorous ruler, he died after eating a 'surfeit of lampreys' at St Denis-le-Fremont, Angers.

30. Remains of the south transept of Reading Abbey. The burial place of Henry I probably lay beyond the wall behind.

Interment and tomb

Henry I's body lay in the quire of St Stephen's Abbey at Caen for four weeks until the wind proved favourable to its transport to England. The body had been eviscerated and had its brain and eyes removed; the skin of the corpse was then gashed, saturated in salt and spices, before being sewn into the hide of a bull. The embalming was not, however, particularly efficacious, black matter flowing from the body during its lying in state. The king's heart, eyes, brain and intestines were buried at Notre Dame des Pres, Rouen, and a monument erected above them. Although Rouen was keen to claim the body as well, it was indeed sent to England, and greeted on arrival by King Stephen. It was buried at Reading Abbey, before the high altar. The tomb was subsequently adorned with a recumbent figure.

Post-interment history

Henry's tomb is known to have been repaired in 1397; however, Reading Abbey was destroyed at the dissolution of the monasteries and the tomb lost. A sixteenth-century tradition that King Henry was buried in a silver coffin allegedly led to the workmen demolishing the quire of the abbey to break into Henry's tomb and in their disappointment scattering the remains. In 1785, a vault and lead coffin thought to be the king's were found, but proved to be from a grave outside the church. Fragments possibly deriving from a stone tomb were found in 1815 and 1989. A small plaque lies in the former area of the south transept, near the site of the tomb, while a large memorial cross lies in the Forbury Gardens.

HOUSE OF BLOIS

STEPHEN (*c.* 1100–1154; r. 1135–1141 & 1141–1154)
Henry I had intended that his daughter, Matilda, succeed him, but instead Stephen, his nephew, succeeded in having himself elected king in London. However, civil war ensued until after the death of Stephen's eldest son, Eustace. Stephen recognised Matilda's son, Henry (II), as his heir.

Interment and tomb
Stephen, his wife and eldest son were all buried in Faversham Abbey, his own foundation. The principal tombs seem to have included a pair of subterranean vaults, each originally around 2.2 metres square, with their floors a similar depth below the pavement. Some fragments found inside may have come from the monuments above, including some finely carved pieces painted red, white, gold and purple.

Post-interment history
Faversham Abbey was demolished in 1539, and Stephen's bones said to have been thrown into the 'next water'. However, a local tradition has it that a canopy tomb with no contemporary inscription in the Trinity Chapel of the nearby parish church of St Mary of Charity marks the king's ultimate resting place.

The site of the abbey was excavated in 1964 and a pair of deep pits identified as probable parts of the royal tombs. It is now covered by the grounds of the Queen Elizabeth II School and by housing.

HOUSE OF NORMANDY

MATILDA (1102–1167; r. 1141)
The only surviving child and heir of Henry I, Matilda (also known as Maud) briefly seized power from Stephen in 1141. Withdrawing to Normandy in 1142, she died at Rouen.

Interment and tomb
Like that of her father, the body of Matilda was wrapped in ox-hide when prepared for burial. She was buried in Bec Abbey; the inscription on her tomb

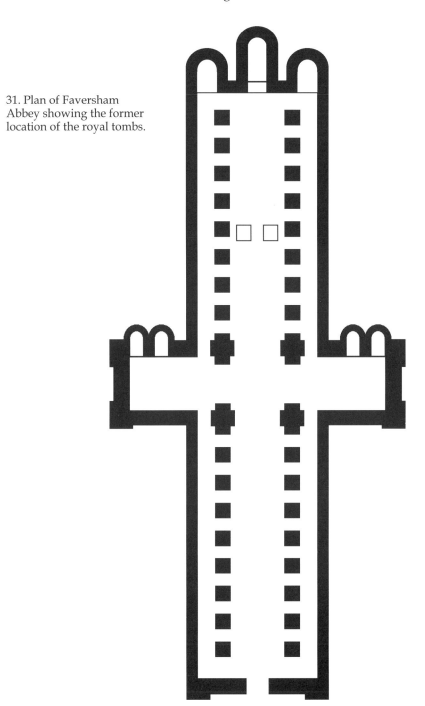

31. Plan of Faversham
Abbey showing the former
location of the royal tombs.

read: 'Here lies Henry's daughter, wife and mother; great by birth, greater by marriage, but greatest by motherhood.' It seems that some portion of her body was also interred at Reading, alongside her father.

Post-interment history

The body was revealed during a rebuilding of the church in 1282, at which time the tomb was moved to the centre of the chancel, before the high altar. The tomb was destroyed by the soldiers of Henry V, but Matilda's presumed bones were found during repairs in 1684 and buried behind the high altar in a lead-covered wooden box. A new monument was provided during the eighteenth century, but Bec Abbey was largely destroyed during the French Revolution. Matilda's remains were, however, rediscovered in 1846, and reinterred in Rouen Cathedral.

HOUSE OF PLANTAGENET

HENRY II (1133–1189; r. 1154–1189)

The son of Matilda, Henry II died on 6 July 1189 at Chinon Castle, France, in the latest in a series of rebellions by his sons.

Interment and tomb

The king had desired to be buried at Grandmont in the Limousin area of France, and work had begun for a tomb in 1170. However, he was in fact buried at Fontevraud Abbey, Normandy, near his place of death, Chinon, clad in the full royal robes. His tomb was in the last bay of the nave of the church, topped by a painted recumbent effigy. Its precise location cannot be determined, but the discovery of the tomb of his grandson, Raymond VII of

32. Tomb-effigy of Henry II, Fontevraud Abbey.

Toulouse, close to the north-west pillar at the junction of the nave and transept in 1985, allowed the area of the original royal cemetery to be defined. Unfortunately, the building of a crypt for the abbesses in 1638 destroyed any trace of the original tomb.

Post-interment history

In 1504 Henry's tomb was moved, along with the other royal tombs in the church, to lie side-by-side in a line towards the northern transept.

In 1638 the tomb was moved again, the effigy being placed above a new monument within an elaborate niche alongside those of Richard I and Queens Eleanor of Aquitaine and Isabella of Angoulême, and kneeling statues of Joan Plantagenet and Raymond VII. The latter replaced earlier effigies; Henry's body was apparently buried nearby.

The abbey and tombs were ransacked in 1793, but one account states that no bones were found at the time. The effigies were dumped in the abbey crypt. They were rediscovered and drawn there by Charles Stothard in 1816. After 1830, Louis-Philippe of France had them taken to Versailles, but they were taken back to Fontevraud in 1849. Napoleon III offered them to Britain, but various French legal objections led to Victoria withdrawing her earlier acceptance of the Emperor's offer. The effigies were reinstalled in the south transept of the abbey church, and moved to their approximate original locations in the 1990s.

Henry II's heart was allegedly salvaged in 1793, but there is no evidence for this having been buried separately, and this may actually have been the heart of Henry III (q.v.).

RICHARD I (1157–1199; r. 1189–1199)

The third son of Henry II, Richard spent only a few months in England, spending much of his time on Crusade or fighting in France, where he died of gangrene following an arrow-wound at Chalus – to which town he bequeathed his bowels.

Interment and tomb

On his death-bed, Richard declared: 'my corpse will be buried in Fontevrault, my heart in Rouen, and my bowels will stay in Chalus.' The Fontevraud tomb comprised a painted recumbent figure, commissioned by his mother, Eleanor, placed at the foot of that of his father. The heart was buried under a monument protected by a 'balustrade of silver' at Rouen, enclosed in two boxes of lead. The viscera went to the church within the fortress at Chalus.

33. Tomb of Richard I, Fontevraud Abbey.

34. Interior of Rouen Cathedral

35. Effigy placed above the heart of Richard I at Rouen.

36. Inscription on the heart container of Richard I.

Post-interment history

The Rouen monument lost its silver in 1250 to help pay the ransom of Louis IX, following his capture during the Crusades. It was replaced by a recumbent effigy, on a table supported by four lions. It suffered some damage at the hands of the Calvinists in 1562 and was demolished during rebuilding in 1734; the spot was marked by a lozenge-shaped slab. The effigy, however, was found under the floor of the quire by Achille Deville on 30 July 1838, buried in cement, 60 centimetres below the surface; its painting and gilding were partly intact. The heart was found in a closed cavity in the adjoining lateral wall, which had been added during the reconstruction. The heart was revealed the next day, encased in two leaden boxes, and examined anatomically on 19 December 1844. Restored by the sculptor Bonet, and reinstalled in the cathedral in 1869, the effigy was moved again in 1956, the base also being lowered; it now lies in the south ambulatory.

37. Tomb of John at Worcester; the tomb-chest and effigy date to Tudor times, when the chantry of Arthur, elder brother of Henry VIII, was built to the south-east.

The tomb at Fontevraud suffered the same fate as that of Henry II, while the Chalus fortress and its church are now in ruins and have never been excavated.

JOHN (1167?–1216; r. 1199–1216)
The youngest son of Henry II, John spent much of his career in conflict with the nobility, and was still so engaged when he died at Newark, Lincolnshire, on 18/19 October 1216 – from dysentery, although poisoning has been alleged.

Interment and tomb
The body was embalmed by the Abbot of Croxton Abbey, Staffordshire, where the viscera were interred. His heart was placed in a gold vessel at Fontevraud. The body was placed in a trapezoid stone coffin, with a round head-cavity, initially placed in the floor of the lady chapel of Worcester Cathedral, between SS Wulfstan and Oswald.

Post-interment history
The body was moved to a new location before the high altar of the cathedral in 1232, at which point an effigy carved out of the original coffin lid was placed on top of the tomb. The tomb was rebuilt as a table-tomb in 1529, the stone coffin being surrounded by new side walls, its lid and effigy being placed atop the new monument. The body-cavity of the stone coffin was

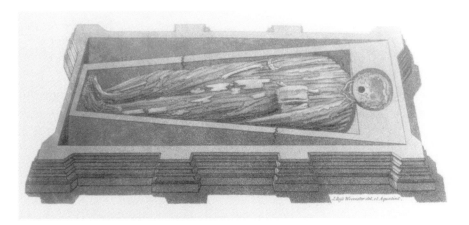

38. John's body as revealed in 1797.

covered with two planks of elm, and two brick cross-walls were laid across the coffin-box to help support the raised lid; the voids were filled with rubble, bricks and plaster. At this time the body was seen to be wrapped in gold and silver cloth, equipped with various regalia, but may have been desecrated during the Civil War.

The tomb was opened in July 1797. During its removal from its original burial place, the body had been disturbed, the cranium becoming turned so that the foramen magnum was uppermost. Both jaws were broken away, the upper lying by the right elbow, and the lower some way from its correct place; the left ulna was also detached.

The treatment of the body is interesting in that, rather than being buried in the royal regalia, as was usual (see Edward I), the king wore a monk's habit, including a cowl, tied under the chin – perhaps to atone for his many sins? Preservation of these robes was fairly good, much of the skeleton being concealed by them. No flesh is reported by the investigator, but he does note two or three handfuls of the dried skins of maggots, which would suggest that the embalming may not have been particularly efficacious.

The king's effigy was gilded during 1873–74, and given a gilt crown. It was restored to its original state in 1930.

HOUSE OF CAPET

LOUIS (1187–1226; r. 1216–1217)
Son and heir of Philippe II of France, Louis was invited to take the throne by English nobles in rebellion against John, and invaded England in May 1216. Defeated at Lincoln in the following year, he resigned his claim under the

Treaty of Lambeth in September 1217. He became King of France as Louis VIII in 1223.

Interment and tomb
Louis was buried at St Denis, 17 kilometres north of Paris; his tomb originally lay behind the matutinal altar.

Post-intermet history
The royal tombs at St Denis were wrecked in 1793, that of Louis being among those entirely lost. The bones of those buried there were dumped in a pit in the Valois cemetery, but recovered in 1817 and buried all together in a small room in the crypt, behind two marble plates bearing the names of all those once interred in the basilica.

HOUSE OF PLANTAGENET

HENRY III (1207–1272; r. 1216–1272)
John's son Henry's long reign included conflict with the barons and religious authorities. He undertook the complete rebuilding of Westminster Abbey and died nearby, in Westminster Palace, on 16 November 1272.

Interment and tomb
At his death, Henry's body was temporarily buried in the former grave of Edward the Confessor, vacated by his translation to its nearby shrine. It was ultimately buried on 10 May 1290 in a tomb constructed by Edward I directly north of the shrine. The image, probably installed in 1292, was made by William Torel, a London goldsmith and, at 5-10 centimetres thick, is more massive than later examples. The right hand had been made separately, the effigy having been cast rather like a bell.

The effigy lay on a table-tomb with a lower section visible from the ambulatory. Much of the exterior was adorned with coloured marbles and multi-coloured (including gilded glass) mosaic, made by the same craftsmen who had constructed the new shrine of Edward the Confessor. The oak coffin, 1.87 metres long, was lowered into place with chains (still in situ) and covered with cloth of gold. It sloped down from the head towards the foot.

Henry's heart was handed over to the Abbess of Fontevraud at the time of his reburial in 1290, and was interred in the abbey there.

39. Tomb of Henry III, as seen from the Confessor's Chapel, Westminster Abbey. Although the main slabs of coloured marble are still in place, most of the multi-coloured mosaic work which covered the remainder of the tomb-chest and its podium is now lost.

40. Effigy of Henry III.

41. Probable heart of
Henry III.

Post-interment history

A painted inscription was added to the Westminster tomb naming the king in 1555–60. Henry III's tomb was opened and examined in 1871, but the wooden coffin was not disturbed. A heart of 'Henry II' – but more probably of Henry III – was allegedly salvaged from the sack of Fontevraud in 1793, and passed through various private hands until acquired by the museum of the municipality of Orléans in 1825. It comprised a desiccated heart in a two-piece leaden, heart-shaped case. In 1857 it was presented to Bishop James Gillis, Vicar-Apostolic of Eastern Scotland, with a view to burial at Westminster, but such an interment was refused by Lord Palmerston, the Prime Minister. In 1864 it was bequeathed to the Congregation of the Ursulines of Jesus, St Margaret's Convent, Edinburgh, where it remains.

EDWARD I (1239–1307; r. 1272–1307)

An effective ruler, Henry III's son spent much of his reign engaged in warfare, particularly in Wales and Scotland; he died on 7 July 1307 at Burgh-on-the-Sands, near Carlisle, while on his way to fight Robert I (the Bruce).

42. Tomb of Edward I as seen from the ambulatory, Westminster Abbey.

Interment and tomb

The king's body lay at Waltham Abbey for sixteen weeks prior to burial. Edward's own wish was that his body should be boiled to allow the bones to be carried on future military expeditions to Scotland, and that his heart should be carried on Crusade. Instead, it was embalmed and placed in a rectangular black Purbeck marble sarcophagus in the north-west corner of the chapel of Edward the Confessor in Westminster Abbey, immediately west of the tomb of Henry III. Although for some reason of very simple form, and not equipped with an effigy nor any carvings or lapidary, the tomb was once in part gilded and sheltered by a massive canopy of wood.

The tomb is 3 metres long and 1.09 metres high, made up of five slabs – four sides and a lid. The cover was not cemented on. It contained a Purbeck marble inner coffin, lying on a bed of rubble. Its walls were 8 centimetres thick, 2 metres long, 40 centimetres high, with a maximum width of 79 centimetres, its surface treated with a yellow paint or varnish. The head-end of the coffin was hollowed out to accept the king's silver gilt crown. The body was wrapped in a coarse, thick, linen cloth, with a three-fold red face-cloth. The body was dressed in its robes, holding a sceptre in each hand.

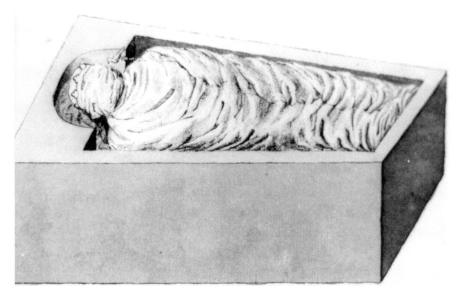

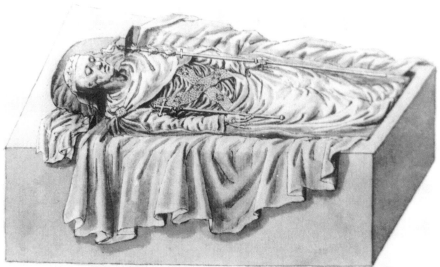

43, 44. Body of Edward I as revealed in 1774.

Post-interment history

The wax of Edward I's cerecloth was renewed regularly until Richard II's reign and in 1555–60 an inscription was added naming the king, together with his epithet 'Scotorum malleus' – 'Hammer of the Scots'. The wooden canopy above the tomb was destroyed in 1764 during a riot that accompanied the funeral nearby of William Pulteney, Earl of Bath.

The tomb was opened and its contents examined in detail in 1774. The face-cloth was badly decayed, but the body itself was well preserved, the flesh still intact, including the form of the chin and lips, although of a very dark colour and somewhat emaciated. Black dust lay below the chin. Although one joint of the middle finger of the right hand was loose, the left hand was quite perfect. After the examination, the coffin and sarcophagus lids were cemented in place to prevent further access. Horace Walpole claimed that pitch was poured on the corpse, but he was not actually present and seems to have been pursuing something of a vendetta against the Society of Antiquaries, which sponsored the opening of the sarcophagus.

EDWARD II (1284–1327; r. 1307–1327)

Created the first Prince of Wales by his father Edward I in 1301, Edward II came to the throne in 1307. His reign was marred by repeated rebellion and defeat in Scotland. He ultimately abdicated and was imprisoned at Berkeley Castle, Gloucestershire, where he died, probably murdered, on 20 January 1327. There has been a suggestion that that the king actually escaped and henceforth lived, and died, in Italy, being buried in the church of Sant Alberto di Butrio, Lombardy.

Interment and tomb

Both Malmesbury and Bristol Abbeys allegedly refused the body of the dead king. However, it was accepted by Gloucester, which had previously enjoyed his benefactions. A magnificent tomb was erected by Edward III on the north side of the sanctuary, a tomb-chest of Purbeck marble topped by an alabaster effigy, sheltered by an arched canopy of oolitic limestone. The king's heart was allegedly ultimately buried in Queen Isabella's coffin in the Grey Friars Church, Newgate.

Post-interment history

The king's outer wooden coffin, lying directly below the tomb-chest, was opened on 2 October 1855, but the inner leaden case, with a flat bottom and a single sheet bent over the body, was not disturbed.

EDWARD III (1312–1377; r. 1327–1377)

The eldest son of Edward II, Edward gave up his predecessors' claim to Scotland, but fought a long war against France, much of it prosecuted by his son, Edward, Prince of Wales (the 'Black Prince'). The founder of the Order of the Garter, the king died at Sheen Palace, Surrey, on 21 June 1377.

45. Tomb of Edward II, Gloucester Cathedral.

Interment and tomb

Edward III was buried in Westminster Abbey, directly south of the Confessor's shrine. The tomb was made of Purbeck marble, the long sides both having six niches, each containing a bronze figure of one of the king's children. The bronze effigy of the king on top, some 12 to 19 mm thick, seems to have been made by John of Liège, and is sheltered by a wooden canopy.

Post-interment history

The king has never been disturbed.

46. Tomb of Edward III as seen from the ambulatory, Westminster Abbey. The figures are those of Edward, Prince of Wales; Joan of the Tower; Lionel, Duke of Clarence; Edmund, Duke of York; Mary of Brittany; William of Hatfield. The corresponding figures on the north side of the tomb are now lost.

47. Head of the effigy of Edward III.

RICHARD II (1367–1400; r. 1377–1399)

The grandson of Edward III by his eldest son, Edward, Prince of Wales, Richard became king while yet a child, and ultimately abdicated in face of the revolt of Henry, Duke of Lancaster and Hereford (Henry IV). The ex-king was then imprisoned 'in perpetuity' at Pontefract Castle, Yorkshire, where he died on 14 February 1400. It has been generally assumed that he was murdered, but examination of Richard's skull found no sign of a wound.

Interment and tomb

During his lifetime, Richard had begun a tomb for himself and his first wife, Anne of Bohemia, at the foot of that of Edward III, moving the tomb of Hugh and Mary de Bohun, grandchildren of Edward I, to make space. Built by the master masons Henry Yevele and Stephen Lote, the tomb was completed in 1397. The tomb was topped by bronze effigies of the king and queen, cast by Nicholas Broker and Godfrey Prest. Trouble had been experienced with casting Anne's image. A large part of the front of the body had had to be re-cast by running fresh metal into the mould, where it fused onto the portion already cast. Richard II's head was cast as a separate piece. The effigies were elaborately adorned with heraldic elements.

48. Tomb of Richard II, as seen from the Confessor's Chapel, Westminster Abbey.

The lower part of the tomb was innovative in that rather than lying in the table-tomb itself, the bodies were to be placed in an arched chamber in its substructure, its floor lying 75 centimetres below the floor of the Confessor's chapel.

In his will, Richard had directed that he should be buried dressed in either velvet or white satin, with a crown and sceptre, together with a ring bearing a precious stone. However, following his abdication and death, the corpse was exposed at St Paul's for three days, embalmed and coffined in lead, except for his exposed face. It was then buried in the priory church of the Friars Preachers, King's Langley, Hertfordshire, apparently with minimal ceremony.

Post-interment history

Henry V had the body exhumed from King's Langley in 1413 and interred in Richard's own tomb at Westminster. Later removal of a series of metal plaques from the substructure of the tomb, which faced out into the ambulatory, resulted in the exposure of the burial cavity to curious hands, who removed a number of items, including Richard's mandible in 1766. Before the openings left by the loss of the plaques were blocked up, the bones were summarily examined by Edward King and Sir Joseph Ayloffe around 1780, who noted a pair of copper crowns.

A scientific investigation led by Dean Stanley was undertaken in August 1871. Inside were found the broken and rotted boards of coffins, with the royal bones in some disarray, with the skulls lying towards the bodies' feet, although most of the king could be seen as lying on the north side of the burial chamber, with most of his lady to the south. Both lower jaws were missing, as were the copper crowns seen in the past. Among the remaining material was a set of iron plumber's shears, possibly used to open the original lead coffin at the time of the reburial in 1413, together with the king's staff, two pairs of gloves, small fragments of the silken pall and nails from the coffins. When examined, the skulls still contained elements of desiccated brain, that of the king described as like 'two walnuts united'. After examination, the bones were placed in their correct relative order in a single sub-divided chest, with other boxes for the other material.

In 1905, Richard II's mandible was returned by the Rev G.T. Andrews, who had received it from an uncle, who had been a schoolboy at the time of the theft. Permission to place it in the tomb was granted by Edward VII on 28 January 1906. At 5 pm on 26 February 1906, the third shield hole from the east was opened, the bone inserted, wrapped in linen, with a note of the event, and the hole sealed. R.B. Seymour undertook an anatomical report on the jaw.

49. Skull of Richard II.

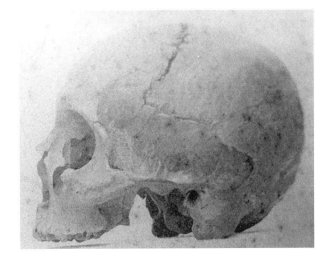

HOUSE OF LANCASTER

HENRY IV (1366–1413; r. 1399–1413)
The son of John of Gaunt, and so grandson of Edward III, Henry returned from banishment to seize the crown. He was taken ill while praying at the Confessor's Chapel in Westminster Abbey, and died in the Jerusalem Chamber there on 20 March 1413.

Interment and tomb
Possibly owing to a lack of space around the Confessor's shrine at Westminster, Henry was buried on the west side of the Trinity Chapel in Canterbury Cathedral, opposite the tomb of the Black Prince, father of his opponent, Richard II. A manuscript account by one Clement Maidestone alleged that while being conveyed between Barking and Gravesend, the boat carrying the king's body had been in caught in a storm and that superstitious seamen had thrown it overboard as a bringer of bad luck; although unlikely in the extreme, this provided the excuse for the later investigation of the king's tomb. Henry's monument, generally regarded as having been erected by Queen Joan after his death, was made by Henry Yevele and was of similar design to those of his immediate predecessors, but with painted alabaster effigies of the king and Queen Joan replacing the metal ones of the earlier monarchs. The tombs was surrounded by a stout iron railing.

Post-interment history
Prompted by doubts as to the actuality of Henry's interment, J.H. Spry began work on 21 August 1832 to verify whether there was a body in the royal coffin.

50. Effigies of Henry IV and Queen Joan in Canterbury Cathedral.

A rough coffin was found lying two-thirds under the west end of the king's monument. Fully under the latter, and on top of the rough coffin, was a simple lead coffin, of two plates soldered together along either side of the body. This was not opened, but was assumed to belong to Queen Joan.

The end of the lid of the 3.5 centimetre thick wooden coffin was sawn off, revealing packing, a cross of twigs and, under these, a lead coffin. This was of semi-anthropoid shape, with a raised section on the torso that might have been intended to house hands in the posture of prayer. An 18 x 10 centimetre oval cut-out having been made, five layers of leather wrappers were revealed. These were still firm and moist, and beneath them was seen the lower part of the perfectly preserved face of the king. His nose shrivelled during the examination, but the bearded chin was still moist, and the eyeballs could be felt when a hand was inserted. The wrappers were then replaced and the coffin re-sealed.

HENRY V (1387–1422; r. 1413–1422)

The eldest son of Henry IV, Henry began a series of campaigns in France in 1415, winning a major victory at Agincourt that year. Having been recognised as heir to the French throne, he died of dysentery at Bois de Vincennes on 31 August 1422.

51. A key element of Henry V's monument in Westminster Abbey is the superb set of iron gates below his chantry, behind which lies the king's tomb-chest.

Interment and tomb

The king's body was eviscerated, and the corpse then cut into pieces and boiled in wine or vinegar; the resulting flesh and bones were mixed with spices and laid in state at St Denis. The viscera were placed in a lead pot which, after pouring the liquid into the adjacent ground, was interred in the church of St Nicholas at St Maur des Fosses, some 10 km south-east of Paris.

Claims were made by both Paris and Rouen as potential burial places for the king, but Henry's 1415 will prevailed and he was interred on 7 November 1422 at Westminster. His tomb was placed at the very eastern end of the Confessor's Chapel, the relics of saints previously housed there being moved to a new location between the tombs of the Confessor and Henry III, and the platform extended eastwards. The table tomb, completed in 1431, was made of Caen stone lined with Purbeck marble, the sides of the chest being decorated with a series of recesses. The upper surface comprised a single piece of oak, the effigy being carved from the same material, and plated with silver; solid silver hands and head were fitted.

Above the tomb, the king had decreed the construction of an elaborately carved chantry chapel, construction of which began in 1438, under the supervision of John Thirske. It was dedicated in 1448. Over the whole were suspended Henry's shield, helmet and saddle.

Post-interment history

A painted inscription was added around the tomb in 1555–60, but pilfering of the precious metal of the effigy began as early as 1467, and in 1546 the head, hands and plating were also stolen. The head was replaced with a resin one in 1971, when his helmet and other relics were removed to the abbey museum. The iron railing that originally protected the eastern end of the tomb was removed in 1822. The chantry chapel ultimately became the burial place of Queen Catherine de Valois in 1878 (see p. 155).

HENRY VI (1421–1471; r. 1422–1461 & 1470–1471)

On his father's premature death, Henry VI was less than a year old. After Edward IV seized the throne in 1461, Henry took refuge in Scotland, but returned to England where he was captured and imprisoned in the Tower of London during 1465–70.

Henry was briefly restored in 1470, but was captured the following year by Edward IV at Barnet, and returned to the Tower, where he died, probably murdered, around 21 May 1471.

Interment and tomb

Henry had planned to be buried at Westminster, between the tombs of Edward the Confessor and Henry III. However, following his death, his body was carried in an open coffin to St Paul's and thence to Blackfriars, allegedly bleeding at both places. From Blackfriars a boat carried the body to Chertsey

52. Henry V's tomb, with its massive oak effigy, lies at the furthest extremity of the Confessor's Chapel overlooking the way into Henry VII's Chapel.

Abbey where it was interred in the lady chapel. According to the 1471 Issue Roll, the wax, linen and spices for the burial of Henry VI cost £15 3s 6^1/2d.

Post-interment history

At Chertsey Henry's body became an object of pilgrimage. Subsequently, Richard III had it exhumed on 12 August 1484 – allegedly perfectly preserved – and taken to St George's Chapel, Windsor. There it was interred just south-west of the altar, on the opposite side to Henry's great enemy, Edward IV.

Under Henry VII, plans were made to rebuild what is now the Albert Chapel at Windsor to hold the remains, but these were opposed by Chertsey and Westminster Abbeys, both of which claimed the body. Ultimately, it was decided that it should be translated to Westminster and buried in a reconstructed lady chapel, the pope having promised that the king would be made a saint. At least two designs were prepared for a new tomb, one with a plain tomb-chest and canopy, and another with a chest topped by an effigy. However, nothing was done, and the body remained at Windsor.

Henry VI's vault was located in 1786 but not opened, an inscribed slab being placed in the floor of the aisle some distance away by Henry Emlyn in 1790. In January 1910 the brick vault was opened and a small lead chest was found among rubbish that included the iron straps from a completely decayed

53. Henry VI's final resting place at Windsor.

coffin, some 2 metres long and 1 metre wide. The chest was investigated on 4 November 1910 and found to hold a decayed wooden box, in which lay disordered human bones. The body had been dismembered before being placed in the chest, the skull being broken and the right arm missing. The remains were accompanied by the humerus of a small pig. Brown hair was still attached to part of the skull, part being rather darker, and conceivably matted with blood. The chest was then repaired and the bones replaced within, wrapped in silk and in a new wooden box, along with the fragments of the old box and ironwork. The bones had every appearance of having once lain in an earthen grave, presumably at Chertsey. The marking slab was moved to above the vault in 1927.

HOUSE OF YORK

EDWARD IV (1442–1483; r. 1461–1470 & 1471–1483)
The son of Richard, Duke of York, and great-great-grandson of Edward III, Edward IV proclaimed himself king, having defeated the forces of Henry VI's wife, Margaret of Anjou. He was briefly set aside in favour of Henry VI, but soon regained the throne. He died in the Palace of Westminster on 9 April 1483.

Interment and tomb
Unlike most of his predecessors, Edward IV forsook Westminster for his new Chapel of St George at Windsor, at the northern side of the altar. A spacious chantry chapel was constructed above, with windows overlooking the high altar, the eastern of which was replaced under Henry VIII to provide a royal pew for Catherine of Aragon.

An elaborate monument was planned to mark the tomb, with a metal image of the king above another showing him as a dead body, but this was apparently never carried out. The location of the burial was marked by a black marble slab, while a pair of iron gates, made by John Tresilian, seem to have formed part of an enclosure around the jewelled coat of arms which also marked the tomb.

The burial vault was built integral with the structure of the chapel, one of whose pillars was supported on the vault's arch. The vault was 2.75 metres long, 1.4 metres wide and 1.45 metres high at its mid-point, with the floor 2 metres below the pavement of the chapel. In addition to that of the king, it also held the body of his wife.

Post-interment history
The tomb was damaged during the Commonwealth, and was partly

54. Northern aisle of the quire of St George's Chapel, Windsor, the location of the chantry of Edward IV, whose oriel window is at the top. The king's tomb lies directly below, to the right.

55. The oriel windows of Edward IV's chantry overlooking the high altar; the right-hand window was replaced under Henry VIII for the use of Catherine of Aragon.

56. Late eighteenth-century monument to Edward IV.

57. On the other side of the wall lies this iron gate, which originally stood around Edward IV's tomb.

reconstructed by Henry Emlyn in 1789–91. A wall was built above the slab marking the tomb, decorated with a black marble slab bearing the king's name in brass letters. The iron gates were placed on the opposite side of the wall, north of the high altar, and effectively hidden from view.

In 1788 an unsuccessful attempt had been made to find an entrance to the vault from the quire. On 21 March 1789, however, while repair work was being carried out in the floor of the chapel, the vault was uncovered. It had clearly been disturbed at some earlier point, as the discovery of the remains of the coffin, skull and scattered bones of Queen Elizabeth Woodville under an upper layer of bricks and rubble demonstrated. A little below lay the compressed, but generally undamaged coffin of the king; no soft tissues seem to have been preserved on the skeleton, but some long brown hair had fallen off the skull. 6.5 centimetres of liquid lay in the bottom of the coffin, which was at an angle, leaving the feet and lower legs immersed.

EDWARD V (1470–*c.* 1483 or 1485/6; r. 1483)
The eldest son of Edward IV, Edward was soon set aside by Parliament on grounds of the invalidity of the marriage of his parents. He was then confined in the Tower of London and presumably subsequently murdered along with his brother, Richard, Duke of York. It remains uncertain who was responsible for their demise; the traditional culprit is Richard III, but Henry VII is also a credible possibility.

Interment and tomb
As with the date and mode of his death, Edward V's burial place remains obscure.

Possible post-interment history
A chest containing the bones of two children was found in an elm chest under a staircase in the Tower on 17 July 1674. They were identified as those of Edward and Richard and initially buried in General Monck's vault in Henry VII's Chapel in Westminster Abbey. They were then moved to an urn in the north aisle of the chapel in 1678. The urn was opened on 6 July 1933, to reveal the bones lying in an oblong cavity in the urn, with the skulls (one broken) at the top. Three rusted nails lay in the dust at the bottom, while various animal bones were also present. After examination, the human bones were wrapped separately in linen and replaced in the urn on 11 July 1933, along with a record of their examination written in parchment.

58. Urn containing the alleged remains of Edward V and Richard, Duke of York.

RICHARD III (1452–1485; r. 1483–1485)

The younger brother of Edward IV, Richard, Duke of Gloucester set aside his nephew, Edward V, and was offered the crown by Parliament. However, an invasion by the usurping Henry Tudor led to Richard's death at the Battle of Bosworth on 22 August 1485.

59. The Church of the Grey Friars, the burial place of Richard III, has long vanished under Greyfriars and Friar Lane in the centre of Leicester.

Interment and tomb

Richard's body was exposed at Leicester and buried with minimal ceremony in the Church of the Grey Friars in that city. In 1495 Henry VII commissioned an alabaster memorial for the tomb from Walter Hylton of Nottingham, although whether in two or three dimensions is unclear.

Post-interment history

Grey Friars Abbey was destroyed at the dissolution of the monasteries, and nothing definite is known of the fate of Richard's body. An oft-quoted story that his bones were thrown in the River Soar post-dates the alleged events by some 70 years. Another tale that Richard's coffin became a cattle trough is made unlikely by the fact that descriptions seem to refer to a coffin of too early a style. A squat pillar inscribed to mark Richard's burial place was apparently to be seen in the house of Robert Herrick, Mayor of Leicester in 1612. It thus remains possible that the body may still remain in its original position, below the modern street or buildings, near Friar Lane and The Greyfriars. A memorial slab was placed in the floor of the chancel of Leicester Cathedral in 1980.

HOUSE OF TUDOR

HENRY VII (1457–1509; r. 1483–1509)

The great-great-great-grandson of Edward III, Henry held himself to be the Lancastrian heir following the death of Henry VI and successfully usurped the throne from Richard III in 1483. His marriage with Elizabeth of York united the two lines of the royal family, thus ending the 'Wars of the Roses'. Henry died at Richmond Palace, Surrey, on 21 April 1509.

Interment and tomb

Henry VII's original plan was to be interred at Windsor. Work began on rebuilding Henry III's chapel to the east of Edward IV's new chapel as a 'tomb-house', but was never completed. A number of payments were made from 1501 towards the actual monument, but in 1502/3 the material was

60. Enclosure of the tomb of Henry VII, Westminster Abbey.

61. Effigies of
Henry VII and
Elizabeth of York.

62. Foot of the
tomb of Henry VII.

63. Entrance to the vault of Henry VII as revealed in February 1869.

moved to Westminster; these seem to have been parts of the screen that was to surround the tomb.

At Westminster, the old lady chapel was demolished and replaced by a new structure, initially intended also to hold the translated corpse of Henry VI at its far end, with Henry VII's tomb before the altar; ultimately, however, Henry VII's occupied the former position. Made by Pietro Torregiano of Florence, at a total cost of £1,500, the monument comprised a black marble tomb-chest, ornamented with copper-gilt and surmounted by the bronze-gilt recumbent figures of the king and queen. The whole, finished on 5 January 1518–19, was surrounded by a massive brass screen.

Henry and Elizabeth's coffins were placed (hers after initial burial elsewhere in the abbey) in a vault below the monument, 2.7 metres long, 1.5 wide and 1.4 high. Their anthropoid leaden coffins were both adorned with maltese crosses, his also bearing a coffin-plate.

Post-interment history
The vault was opened in 1625 for the burial of James VI & I, during which the wooden outer coffins of both Henry and Elizabeth were stripped off to make room for the additional interment, leaving just the leaden inner cases. It is possible that their visceral urns were moved to the nearby vault of General Monck. The tomb was opened and examined by Dean Stanley in February 1869.

HENRY VIII (1491–1547; r. 1509–1547)
The second, but eldest surviving, son, of Henry VII, Henry's divorce from Catherine of Aragon resulted in the establishment of the independent Church of England, and the dissolution of the monasteries during 1535–39. The latter part of the reign was marked by widespread judicial murder and five further marriages, the king dying at Whitehall Palace on 28 January 1547.

Interment and tomb
On the same day in 1518–19 that the tomb of Henry VII was completed, an indenture was drafted for the making of Henry VIII's monument by Benedetto da Rovezzano, to cost £2,000, and be a quarter larger. Its location was to be determined four years later.

The 'tomb-house' which Henry VII had begun at Windsor was roofed over by his son who, however, then granted it as a sepulchre to his great minister, Cardinal Thomas Wolsey. After Wolsey's fall in 1530, the building reverted to the king, work moving ahead on a structure incorporating both the symbolic sarcophagus already made for the Cardinal, and Henry's original work. The

64. Reconstruction of the intended tomb of Henry VIII in the Albert Chapel at Windsor.

monument was to be a chantry chapel, standing on a platform 8 x 4 metres, surrounded by a bronze enclosure 1.4 metres high. Ten bronze pillars would support 1.5 metre figures of apostles and eight 3 metre candlesticks would surround a podium supporting an (empty) sarcophagus, upon which would lie an effigy of the king.

However, at the king's death it appears that although the podium and sarcophagus were in position, as may have been the recumbent effigy, much of the rest was incomplete. Under his will, Henry therefore directed that he be buried alongside Queen Jane Seymour in a small vault in the quire of St

65. Vault of Henry VIII with, from the left, the coffins of Charles I, Henry VIII and Jane Seymour.

George's Chapel, but that they should be moved to the 'tomb-house' once it was complete.

Thus, after being enclosed in its lead coffin, with an outer one of elm, the body was transported to Windsor, resting at Syon Abbey en route. While there, the coffin is alleged to have burst open, blood being licked from the floor by a dog in fulfilment of a prophesy allegedly made at the time of his divorce from Catherine of Aragon. This should be compared with a similar tale told of the coffin of Elizabeth I (see pp. 96-7). The king's heart and viscera remained in London, being interred in the chapel of Whitehall Palace.

The royal corpse was laid to rest in a vault in the quire, in which Jane Seymour had previously been interred. The original entrance to the vault seems to have been from the west, but the king's coffin is stated to have been lowered from above. The chamber measured 3 metres long by 2.25 metres wide and 1.5 metres high, space being left for (presumably) Queen Catherine Parr. The latter, outliving her husband, was, however, buried at Sudeley Castle, Gloucestershire; 'her' space was to remain vacant until the seventeenth century.

Post-interment history
Further material was moved to Windsor in 1565 and erection begun, but

nothing is recorded as happening after 1572. Although the intention to complete Henry's great tomb remained alive into the reign of Elizabeth I, it never came to pass. All bronze elements were sold off by Parliament in 1646 (four candlesticks are identifiable in the church of St Bavon at Ghent, Flanders), but the podium and sarcophagus seem to have remained in place until the excavation of George III's vault underneath in 1804. The sarcophagus was then installed as the monument above Nelson's grave in the crypt of St Paul's Cathedral, London, in 1808–10, after his funeral in 1806.

Henry VIII's body seems to have remained undisturbed until 1648 (statements that the king's body was burned by Mary I are wholly without foundation). That year, Charles I's burial was made in the vault (see pp. 99-100), and King Henry's 'very thin' leaden covering was casually opened and a yellow powder within examined, while parts of his pall were cut away by a bystander. An 1888 examination claimed that the then-fractured edges of the coffin showed signs of the action of internal force outwards, in which case the coffin may have already been split in 1648.

Although the coffin was supposedly re-closed after this examination, when the tomb was opened in 1813 (see pp. 99-100), the coffin 'appeared to have been beaten in by violence about the middle, thus exposing a mere skeleton of the King'; among other elements visible were parts of his famous beard. Of his 2.1 metre elm outer coffin, only a few fragments remained. It is possible that the further damage to Henry VIII's coffin occurred when an infant of Queen Anne was placed in the vault in the early eighteenth century.

The location of the vault was marked by a marble slab with a text in brass letters in 1837, and was opened twice more, once by accident in 1861, and once to return some relics of Charles I in 1888. On the latter occasion, Henry's coffin was seen to be 'all open at the top so that [one] could see into it, and there lay the bones and the skull of the King'. Fragments of the reddish wood of the former outer coffin, some 5 centimetres thick, were seen strewn around upon the torn lead.

EDWARD VI (1537–1553; r. 1547–1553)
The son of Henry VIII and Jane Seymour, Edward came to throne while yet a child. The reign saw attempts to entrench Protestantism in England, but was cut short by the young king's premature death at Greenwich Palace on 6 July 1553.

Interment and tomb
Edward VI remained unburied for a month, owing to negotiations over the nature of his funeral rights following the accession of his Catholic sister, Mary.

66. Coffin-plate of Edward VI.

67. Reconstruction of the Edward VI altar at Westminster.

His tomb was marked by a fine marble and brass altar by either Torregiano or da Rovezzano. The coffin-plate had, however, been prepared under Jane, and was wholly Protestant in formulation. The body was placed in a small brick-arched vault, 2.3 metres long and 75 centimetres wide, within the entrance-cut of Henry VII's vault. A joint monument for Edward VI and Mary I was later mooted, but nothing was done after 1572, the same year which saw the abandonment of Henry VIII's tomb.

Post-interment history

The altar above the tomb was destroyed by the Puritans in 1643, when the vault may also have been disturbed, fragments of the altar being found in it in 1868. A new altar, by Sir George Gilbert Scott, stood in its former place from 1870 until 1935, when it was replaced by a near-replica of the sixteenth century piece. When examined in 1868, the wooden outer coffin was then found to have been partly cleared away, and the leaden shell seen to be 'rent and deformed as well as wasted by long corrosion'. The state of the coffin allowed contents to be viewed: 'The cerecloth had fallen away, and showed that no hair was attached to the skull.'

HOUSE OF GREY

JANE (1537–1554; r. 1553)

The will of Edward VI attempted to set aside the rights of his sisters Mary and Elizabeth (and of James V of Scotland) in favour of their cousin, Jane Grey, the great-granddaughter of Henry VII. Her 'reign' lasted only nine days, before Mary I was able to assert her rights. Jane was then imprisoned in the Tower and executed on 12 February 1554, following the abortive rebellion of Sir Thomas Wyatt.

Interment and tomb

Jane's body was buried alongside other executed nobility (including Queens Anne Boleyn and Catherine Howard) in the chapel of St Peter ad Vincula in the Tower of London. It has been suggested that her body, and that of her husband, were placed near the north wall of the chancel, but no traces were found when the area was examined in 1876/7.

HOUSE OF TUDOR

MARY I (1516–1558; r. 1553–1558)

The daughter of Henry VIII and Catherine of Aragon, Mary attempted to

68. Monument to Elizabeth I, surmounting her and Mary's tomb at Westminster Abbey.

re-establish Roman Catholicism. Having suffered poor health in her last years, she died at St James's Palace, London, on 17 November 1558.

Interment and tomb
Mary's body was placed in a narrow vault in the north aisle of Henry VII's Chapel at Westminster. The location was marked by stones taken from the Catholic altars in the chapel that were dismantled soon after her death.

Post-interment history
The vault was opened on the death of Elizabeth I, and her coffin placed on top of Mary's. Elizabeth's monument was placed above the vault, Mary being commemorated only by its inscriptions.

Mary's heart was seen in 'General Monck's vault' in the abbey in 1670, during the funeral of George Monck, Duke of Albemarle, himself, when the organ was allegedly handled by a schoolboy named William Taswell.

ELIZABETH I (1533–1603; r. 1558–1603)
The daughter of Henry VIII and Anne Boleyn, Elizabeth's long reign saw many upheavals, including the defeat of the Spanish Armada. She died at Richmond Palace on 24 March 1602–03.

Interment and tomb
The treatment of the queen's body remains slightly uncertain, since she had apparently left instructions that she should not be embalmed. Contradictory accounts exist as to whether her wishes were respected, together with a tale that, while lying in state, the body exploded with such force that the lead coffin split. It seems likely, however, that the latter was actually a

69. Dedication on the tomb of Elizabeth I.

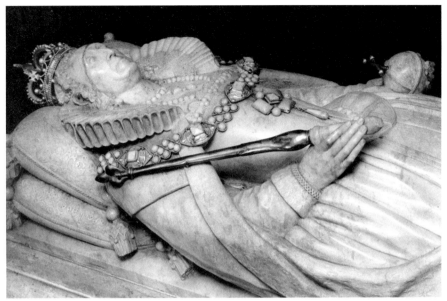

70. Upper part of Elizabeth's effigy.

71. Royal cypher on the lid of Elizabeth's coffin.

Catholic-inspired fiction to suggest that the Protestant Elizabeth's death had been surrounded by ill-omen.

The anthropoid lead shell was enclosed in an elm trough 2.5 centimetres thick, with an oak lid and oak panelling, all covered with red silk velvet, with the Tudor rose and royal cipher on the lid. It lay on top of the coffin of Mary I, a monument being erected above the now joint vault by James VI & I. The latter was the work of M. Colt and J. de Critz, and was completed in 1606, at a cost of £765. It bears an recumbent effigy of the queen, with a heavily ornamented arched superstructure.

Post-interment history

The monument was despoiled of some of its adornments before 1763, replaced by new items during 1975–88. The coffin was briefly examined during Stanley's work in Westminster Abbey in 1868. Like that of her sister Mary, the queen's heart was seen in 'General Monck's vault' in the abbey in 1670.

HOUSE OF STUART

JAMES I (1566–1625; also James VI of Scotland: r. in Scotland 1567–1625; r. in England 1603–1625)

The son of Mary, Queen of Scots, and Henry, Lord Darnley, James succeeded to the Scots throne as a baby on his mother's abdication. His early life was turbulent. He obtained the English throne as great-great-grandson of Henry VII. James died at Theobalds Park, Hertfordshire, on 27 March 1625.

Interment and tomb

James was buried in the vault of Henry VII himself, in an anthropoid leaden case, enclosed in a massive wooden coffin hollowed out of two logs of solid timber. To make room for this, the wooden cases of Henry VII and Queen Elizabeth of York had been cleared away, and the latter's lead shell temporarily stacked upon her husband's. It is possible that the visceral urns of all three occupants were placed in the vault of General Monck, where lay that of Queen Anne of Denmark.

A scheme existed for the erection of a classically-styled monument to the king, but nothing was ever done.

Post-interment history

The vault was examined by Dean Stanley in February 1869.

CHARLES I (1600–1649; also of Scotland; r. 1625–1649)

Charles was the younger son of James I. Following disputes over religious and political issues in both kingdoms, Charles initiated the English Civil War against Parliament in 1642. Captured by the Scots in 1646, he was ultimately executed at Whitehall Palace on 30 January 1649.

72. Vault of Henry VII with, from the left, the leaden coffins of
James I, Henry VII and Elizabeth of York.

Interment and tomb

Following the reattachment of the head and embalming of the corpse, its
cheap wooden coffin was sealed inside a leaden case and carried to St James's
Palace. Parliament then determined that Charles should be buried at Windsor,
within the secure walls of the Castle, to avoid any chance of his tomb
becoming the focus of pilgrimages or demonstrations. He was moved to
Windsor a week after the execution. Locations considered by those charged
with the burial included the unused 'tomb-house' of Wolsey and Henry VIII,

and a site adjacent to the tomb of Edward IV. However, the coffin was ultimately interred inside the vault of Henry VIII, in the centre of the quire, at the earlier king's right hand. To gain access, it appears that the west end of the vault was partly pulled down and then roughly blocked with fragments of bricks and masonry.

Post-interment history

Following the Restoration, consideration was given to a reburial of Charles's remains, possibly in the rebuilt St Paul's, or at Westminster. The final plan was to demolish the Windsor 'tomb-house' and replace it with a circular domed mausoleum designed in classical style by Sir Christopher Wren. However, nothing was ever done, owing to a failure to obtain funds before the death of Charles II.

The coffin of a still-born child of Anne was placed upon the king's coffin in 1696, which remained undisturbed until March 1813. Then, during work connected with the new royal vault, the old vault was penetrated. It was decided that Charles I's coffin should be opened under the direction of Sir Henry Halford, the Prince Regent's doctor.

An opening was specially made in the upper part of the lead coffin, revealing the badly decayed inner coffin. The head was removed from the coffin, the flesh and hair of which were found to be still intact, with the skin 'dark and discoloured. The forehead and temple had but little or nothing of their muscular substance, the cartilage of the nose was gone'. The left eye was open and full when exposed, but disappeared immediately afterwards. The head lay in a fluid, which may represent the residues of the spirits of wine used in the embalming process.

After the examination, the head was replaced and the leaden coffin soldered up. Certain items were removed by Halford, including part of the king's hair and beard, part of a cervical vertebra and a tooth. These were ultimately handed over to Albert Edward, Prince of Wales, by Halford's grandson in 1888. Their casket was placed in a leaden box and introduced into the vault via a 45 centimetre hole in the roof on 13 December 1888, being lowered into place by the Prince himself, using a handkerchief belonging to A.Y. Nutt, the Surveyor to the Dean and Chapter.

THE COMMONWEALTH

OLIVER CROMWELL (1599–1658; in office 1653–1658)
Cromwell was elected MP for Huntingdon in 1628 and for Cambridge in 1640. He played a leading role in the Civil War and in the administration of the

resulting Commonwealth. In 1653 he became formally Lord Protector with supreme power, refusing in 1657 an offer of the royal crown itself. He died at Whitehall Palace on 3 September 1658.

Interment and tomb
The Protector was interred in a large vault constructed for him at the easternmost end of Henry VII's Chapel at Westminster. It is possible that he was actually buried there some time before his formal funeral on 23 November.

Post-interment history
On 26 January 1661, six months after the restoration of Charles II, Cromwell's body was disinterred, along with those of those of two others who had signed Charles I's death warrant. Cromwell's vault was subsequently used for the interment of illegitimate descendants of Charles II, and then for various notables, beginning with the Duke of Ormonde and his family in the 1680s.

On 30 January 1661 the disinterred corpses were dragged in their coffins to the gallows at Tyburn. There they were taken out and hung and then decapitated, the heads being placed on poles above Westminster Hall on 5

73. Coffin plate of Oliver Cromwell, ripped from his coffin at its exhumation (on loan to the Museum of London).

February. The coffin-plate of Cromwell is now on loan to the Museum of London. The bodies were buried below the gallows, though there is a story that Cromwell's was rescued by his daughter, Mary, Countess Fauconburg, and buried at Newburgh Priory, North Yorkshire, in a room over the porch of the house.

The head (p. 5 [fig. 3]) remained on its spike until it was blown down in a gale in the 1680s. It then seems to have passed, before 1710, into the 'museum' of Claudius Du Puy, who died in 1738. Around 1775, the head came into the hands of Samuel Russell, an actor, who later offered it to the Master of Sidney Sussex College, Cambridge – Cromwell's Alma Mater. The offer having been declined, Russell ultimately sold the head in 1787 to James Cox, for his 'museum'. In 1799 it was purchased from Cox by James Cranch and two partners for £230 and exhibited in Mead Court, Old Bond Street, London, and later elsewhere. Then, around 1814, Josiah Henry Wilkinson purchased the head from the daughter of the last of Cranch's partners; it remained in the Wilkinson family until the late 1950s. While in their hands, the head was subjected to a scientific examination by Karl Pearson and G.M. Morant in the early 1930s, which verified its authenticity, and that it had been embalmed in accordance with seventeenth-century practice (see p. 7), the brain having been removed by sawing off the skull cap, the process being aided by the use of a chisel on the occipital bone. It had then been sewn back in place, the shrunken leather-like skin of the scalp still preserving the needle holes.

In 1956 the head was housed in a box and wrapped in dark red silk, but at the end of the decade, the son of its last owner, Canon Wilkinson of Ramsholt, Suffolk, presented it to Sidney Sussex College. It was interred in the college chapel on 25 March 1960.

RICHARD CROMWELL (1626–1712; in office 1658–1659)

The son of Oliver, Richard Cromwell was appointed Protector on his father's death, but rapidly fell into dispute with the Army and resigned within a year. Pursued by creditors, he fled to France in 1660 under an assumed name. He returned to England around 1680 and lived in retirement.

Interment and tomb

Richard Cromwell was buried in the chancel of All Saint's Church, Hursley, Hampshire, alongside many of his family and his in-laws. A marble tablet listing them all was added following the death of Richard's daughter, Elizabeth, in 1731.

Post-interment history

The old church, except for the tower, was replaced by a new structure in

74. Chapel of Sidney Sussex College, Cambridge, the last resting place of Cromwell's head.

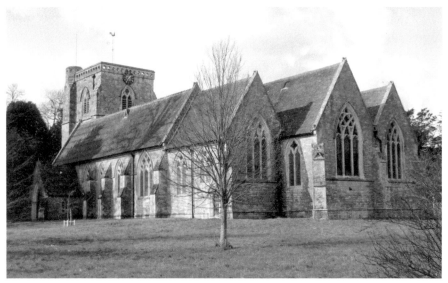

75. Hursley Church, the burial place of Richard Cromwell.

76. Memorial slab of Elizabeth Cromwell, Richard's daughter, listing him among the many members of her family interred in the church.

1752/3. In 1847/8 it was rebuilt by the poet and leading figure of the high church Oxford Movement, John Keble, vicar from 1835 to 1866.

During the latter rebuilding the Cromwell family tablet was removed by the anti-Puritan Keble, but stored by Sir William Heathcote, the local Lord of the Manor, until after Keble's death in 1866, when it was placed under the tower, on the north wall. An additional tablet, naming Richard as Lord Protector, was added next to it by the Cromwell Association in March 1993.

HOUSE OF STUART

CHARLES II (also of Scotland: 1630–1685; r. 1649[*de jure*]/1660[*de facto*]–1685)
The son of Charles I and Queen Henrietta Maria, Charles had attempted to regain his throne in 1650/1, receiving the Scottish crown at Scone, but was forced to retreat to France after defeat at the Battle of Worcester. Following Richard Cromwell's resignation, negotiations with General George Monck (later Duke of Albemarle) resulted in his restoration in May 1660. Charles died at Whitehall Palace on 6 February 1685.

Interment and tomb
Charles II was buried in a vault constructed immediately after his death at the end of the south aisle of the Henry VII Chapel in Westminster Abbey; this was to remain the 'royal vault' until after the interment of Anne. It was

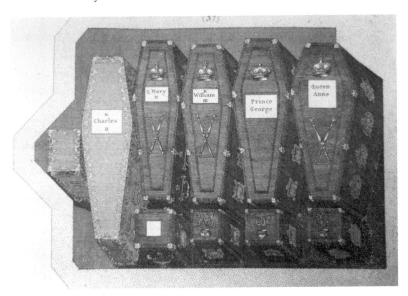

77. The Westminster vault of the Stuarts.

78. Parish church of St Germain-en-Laye, burial place of the viscera of James VII & II.

approached by an incline and flight of five steps under the south-eastern stalls of the Knights of the Bath and the monument of the Duke of Albemarle.

Post-interment history

The entrance to the vault was accidentally rediscovered in 1867 during the installation of heating pipes. Charles II's coffin found was badly decayed, the lead plates having fallen inwards, partly revealing his skull. The vault has been entered on a number of subsequent occasions.

JAMES II (also James VII of Scotland: 1633–1701; r. 1685–1688)

The brother of Charles II, James had previously converted to Catholicism. His attempts to promote his religion and absolute monarchy led to the invasion of William of Orange and James's flight to France. Attempts to regain his throne failed and he died at St Germain-en-Laye, France.

Interment and tomb

In the hope of his line's restoration and his interment in Westminster Abbey, James's body was not buried, being placed in one of the chapels of the Chapel of Saint Edmund in the convent of the English Benedictines in the rue du Faubourg St Jacques in Paris. It lay in an inner wooden coffin, enclosed by one of lead, and an outer wooden one, covered with black velvet. His various organs were distributed around Paris, the brain being placed in a casket on top of an obelisk in the Parisian Scots' College, the heart in the Convent of the Visitandine Nuns at Chaillot (where Queen Mary of Modena was buried), and the viscera divided between the parish church of St Germain-en-Laye and the English Church of St Omer.

Post-interment history

The king's coffins were broken open by French Revolutionaries to get at the lead in 1793/4, and the body left exposed for a day, during which time it was seen to be still well preserved. It was then taken away and not seen again, presumably having suffered the same fate as that of the French kings at St Denis – consignment to the common pit. The other parts of the body also disappeared during the Revolution.

However, the inscribed leaden box holding the St Germain internal organs was one of three such containers found during the digging of foundations for the rebuilding of the ruinous church in 1824. The other two seem to have held viscera of James's wife, Mary of Modena, and their daughter, Louisa; all were

79. Monument to James VII & II erected in the church of St Germain-en-Laye by Victoria.

placed under the altar pending the completion of the new church. The remains were then interred in a coffin which was buried below the altar on 10 September 1824, a plain black marble tablet being placed in front of the altar.

George IV planned to erect a monument in the church, but this was never executed. However, in 1855 Victoria made a visit and subsequently raised a monument to James in a chapel to the right of the entrance to the church. *For 'James III', 'Charles III' and 'Henry IX', see Appendix 2.*

MARY II (also of Scotland: 1662–1694; r. 1689–1694)
The eldest daughter of James VII & II, Mary became joint sovereign with her husband, William III, following his invasion and the flight of her father. She died of smallpox at Kensington Palace.

Interment and tomb
Mary was buried alongside her uncle, Charles II, in the vault in Westminster Abbey. Although drawings were produced for a monument to her, nothing was ever made.

HOUSE OF ORANGE

WILLIAM III (also William II of Scotland and Willem III of United Provinces of the Netherlands: 1650–1702; r. 1689–1702)
The nephew and son-in-law of James VII & II, William landed at Brixham, Devon, and was offered the throne by Parliament. His reign was marked by Jacobite revolts and warfare in Europe. He died at Kensington Palace following a fall from his horse.

Interment and tomb
The king's coffin was placed next to that of his wife. Drawings were made for a joint monument for William and Mary, but nothing was ever constructed.

HOUSE OF STUART

ANNE (also of Scotland, and then of Great Britain from 1707: 1665–1714; r. 1702–1714)
The second daughter of James II, Anne's reign saw continued warfare in Europe and the formal union of England and Scotland in 1707. Anne bore seventeen children, none of whom lived to adulthood, and had poor health, finally dying of kidney failure in London on 1 August 1714.

Interment and tomb
Anne was buried alongside Charles II, Mary II and William III in their Westminster vault.

The thrones of Scotland and England were formally united in 1707.

III

Scotland

HOUSE OF MACALPIN

KENNETH I (r. *c*. 841–*c*. 859)
Kenneth I was in effect the founder of what was to become the Scottish nation. His death appears to have been caused by cancer, at Forteviot, Perthshire. He was buried at Iona.

DONALD I (r. *c*. 859–*c*. 863)
The short reign of this brother of Kenneth I was terminated by a death, at Scone in 863, which may not have been natural. He was buried at Iona.

CONSTANTINE I (r. 863–877)
A son of Kenneth I, Constantine I died fighting against the Danes in Fife, and was buried at Iona.

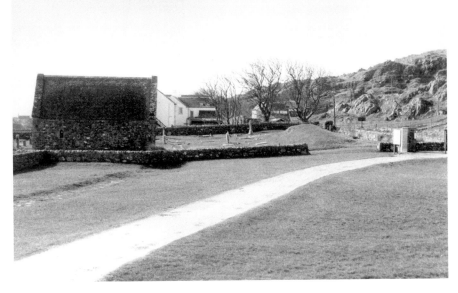

80. The Relig Oran, traditional burial place of the early Scottish kings on Iona.

AEDH (r. 877–878)

The brother of Constantine I, Aedh had his reign cut short when he was killed at Strathallen by Giric, the son of Donald I. He was buried at Iona.

EOCHAID (r. 878–889)
GIRIC I (r. 878–889)

Giric, following his defeat of his cousin, shared the throne with Eochaid. The co-regents were both deposed a decade later, Giric being killed at Dundurn in Perthshire. They are believed to have been buried at Iona.

DONALD II (r. 889–900)

The son of Constantine I, Donald died at Dunnottar or near Forres, possibly having been poisoned. He was buried at Iona.

CONSTANTINE II (d. 952; r. 900–943)

The reign of Constantine, a son of Aedh, ended with the demoralised king's abdication and retreat to the monastery at St Andrews. He was buried there.

MALCOLM I (*c.* 897–954; r. 943–954)

The new king, a son of Donald II, invaded England but was ultimately killed at Fordoun while attempting to put down a revolt in Moray.

Interment and tomb

Malcolm is supposed to have been buried on Iona, like most of his predecessors, but it has been suggested that his sepulchre might have been a tumulus at Fetteresso, Kincardineshire, on the basis of an old chronicle that places Malcolm's death at 'Fodresach in Claideom' – possibly Fetteresso.

Post-interment history

The tumulus was investigated in the early nineteenth century. A stone coffin was found 2 metres below the surface, comprising single slabs and covered with a single stone. The body had been embedded in some vegetable substance and covered with a net, which fell to dust. The legs had been bent back to allow the body to be fitted into the coffin. The flesh of the abdomen and other parts had been converted to adipocere (a cheese-like substance to which soft tissues may be converted after burial in certain conditions). No traces of skull or teeth were found, but over the breast lay a small oval wooden box.

INDULF (r. 954–962)
A son of Constantine II, Indulf's reign ended with his death at the hands of the Norsemen at Invercullen. He was buried on Iona.

DUBH (r. 962–966/7)
The elder son of Malcolm I, Dubh was twice challenged by Indulf's son Culen, on the second occasion being killed at Forres. It is said that until the king's body was found and buried (at Iona), the sun failed to shine – perhaps a reference to the eclipse of 10 July 967.

CULEN (r. 966/7–971)
This monarch was killed in battle by Rhiderch, king of Strathclyde, whose territory he had invaded. He was buried at Iona.

KENNETH II (932–995; r. 971–995)
The second son of Malcolm I, Kenneth lost his life in an uprising and was interred at Iona.

CONSTANTINE III (r. 995–997)
This short reign of a son of Culen was ended by the king's murder in Rathinveramon, and followed by burial at Iona.

GIRIC II (r. 997–1005)
This king ruled alongside his father, Kenneth III, son of Dubh; he was killed at Monzievaird, Perthshire, by Malcolm II. Giric was buried at Iona.

MALCOLM II (*c.* 954–1034; r. 1005–1034)
A son of Kenneth II, Malcolm II established what was henceforth recognised as the border between Scotland and England. He died at Glamis Castle, Angus, perhaps of old age, but possibly of wounds; he was buried at Iona.

HOUSE OF DUNKELD

DUNCAN I (*c.* 1001–1040; r. 1034–1040)
A grandson of Malcolm II, Duncan had been King of Strathclyde since 1018, his accession marking the final union of the two territories. His reign and life were cut short in battle with Macbeth at Bothganowan, Elgin; he was buried at Iona.

MACBETH (r. 1040–1057)

Macbeth appears to have been another grandson of Malcolm II, and grandson-in-law of Kenneth III. Macbeth was killed in battle with the future Malcolm III; he was buried on Iona.

LULACH (*c*. 1032–1058; r. 1057–1058)

Lulach was the stepson of Macbeth, and his reign lasted but four months, being ended by the final victory of Malcolm III. His body was interred on Iona.

MALCOLM III (*c*. 1031–1093; r. 1058–1093)

The son of Duncan I, Malcolm III made numerous forays across the border, until a final Northumbrian adventure brought about his death: the exact circumstances differ between authors.

Interment and tomb

The king's body was buried by Robert de Mowbray in the priory at Tynemouth. During the reign of Alexander I, two bodies were removed from Tynemouth for reburial at Dunfermline as those of Malcolm and his son, Edward. They were placed alongside the grave of Queen Margaret before the Holy Cross altar of the abbey church.

However, two skeletons found over a century later, in 1247, during building work at Tynemouth, were then also identified as the king and his son, and apparently given new tombs in the abbey church. It thus remains uncertain whether Malcolm III's actual body was handed over to Alexander I, or whether it remained in England.

Post-interment history

The supposed remains of the king at Dunfermline were moved by Alexander III around 1250, when those of Malcolm's sainted wife, Margaret, were translated into a new eastern extension of the church. The queen's bones were enshrined in a silver casket, her husband's being added after Margaret allegedly miraculously refused to allow her casket to be carried past Malcolm's tomb in its procession to its new resting place.

After the destruction of the eastern end of the abbey in 1560, including the area of the shrine, some of the remains of the couple were allegedly acquired by Philip II of Spain, who placed them in the church of San Lorenzo in the Escorial palace in two urns. They were disturbed during the French occupation in the early nineteenth century, and when Bishop Gillis applied through Pope Pius IX for the remains' return to Scotland, they could not be identified.

81. Tynemouth Abbey, where some of the early Northumbrian kings had been buried, and where Malcolm III's body was initially interred.

82. Former location of the shrine of St Margaret at Dunfermline, beyond what is now the east end of the church (surrounded by railings).

DONALD III (*c.* 1033–1099; r. 1093–1094 & 1094–1097)

Malcolm III's sibling, Donald, managed to take Edinburgh on his brother's death. However, he was soon deposed by Duncan II, before a counter-coup was mounted by Donald and Edmund, who then ruled together. The co-regents were finally overthrown by Edgar, Donald being blinded and imprisoned, dying at Rescobie, Forfarshire; he was first buried at Dunkeld, his remains being moved to Iona before 1150.

DUNCAN II (*c*. 1060–1094; r. 1094)
A hostage in England since 1072, Malcolm II's son Duncan gained the throne with English backing. His tenure was short. He was killed at Mondynes by Malpei, *mormaer* (high steward) of the Mearns; his burial place is uncertain, although one source places it on Iona.

EDMUND (r. 1094–1097)
As Donald III's co-regent, Edmund, son of Malcolm III, governed the southern part of their realm. After his deposition he retired to an English monastery.

EDGAR (*c*. 1074–1107; r. 1097–1107)
Edgar, a younger son of Malcolm III, was placed on the throne by an English-backed coalition. He died unmarried at either Dundee or Edinburgh.

Interment and tomb
The king was buried at Dunfermline 'before the Great Altar'.

ALEXANDER I (*c*. 1077–1124; r. 1107–1124)
Yet another son of Malcolm III, Alexander shared authority with his brother, David I. On his death at Stirling, the king was without legitimate issue.

Interment and tomb
Buried at Dunfermline 'before the Great Altar'.

DAVID I (*c*. 1080–1153; r. 1124–1153)
The nearly three decades of David's reign marked the consolidation of Scotland as a distinct entity. He died peacefully at Carlisle on 24 May 1153.

Interment and tomb
Buried at Dunfermline 'in the pavement of the middle quire'.

MALCOLM IV (1142–1165; r. 1153–1165)
David I's grandson died young at Jedburgh Castle.

Interment and tomb
Buried at Dunfermline 'before the greater altar in the middle of the pavement'.

83. Romanesque nave of Dunfermline Abbey.

84. Ruins of Arbroath Abbey, burial place of William the Lion.

85. This mutilated effigy may be that of William the Lion.

WILLIAM 'THE LION' (1143–1214; r. 1165–1214)

A brother of Malcolm IV, William was forced to hand over to Henry II a number of castles, including Edinburgh, returned in 1186. The king died at Stirling.

Interment and tomb

William was buried in Arbroath Abbey.

118

Post-interment history

The king's tomb was destroyed at the Reformation; remains of what may have been his effigy are now on display at the abbey ruins.

ALEXANDER II (1198–1249; r. 1214–1249)

The son of William I, Alexander died on the Isle of Kerrara, near Oban.

Interment and tomb

The king was interred near the high altar at Melrose Abbey, Roxburghshire.

86. East end of Melrose Abbey, location of the tomb of Alexander II.

ALEXANDER III (1241–1286; r. 1249–1286)

Coming to the throne as a child, Alexander attended the coronation of his brother-in-law, Edward I of England, and continued peaceful relations with his southern neighbour for the rest of his reign. He died in a riding accident at Kinghorn, Fife.

Interment and tomb

After the removal of his heart for burial in the Church of St John the Baptist at Perth, Alexander was interred at Dunfermline Abbey, in the new eastern extension he had built for the translation of the relics of (Queen) St Margaret in 1250, south-west of the new high altar. The tomb is now lost.

HOUSE OF NORWAY

MARGARET (1283–1290; r. 1286–1290)

The granddaughter of Alexander I, she was the offspring of Alexander's daughter, also named Margaret, who had married Erik II of Norway. Her mother having predeceased Alexander, the younger Margaret was Alexander's only heir. She died on the ship bringing her to her kingdom, paving the way for sixteen years of chaos.

Tomb and interment

Margaret's body was taken back to Norway and buried in the Kristkirken Cathedral in Bergen. This had been completed in the late twelfth century, a massive new royal chapel being added between 1275 and 1302. The cathedral, chapel and the associated monastery were demolished around 1530 to make room for the enlargement of the adjacent castle.

HOUSE OF BALLIOL

JOHN (*c.* 1250–1313; r. 1292–1296)

A great-great-great-grandson of David I, John was chosen as the new king by Edward I who was acting as arbitrator amongst the thirteen claimants. However, his refusal to do the English king's will led to war and his capture and abdication; he died in retirement at Castle Galliard, Normandy.

Interment and tomb

John was buried at Bailleul, in the church of St Waast.

More than 90% of the town was destroyed in April 1918, during the First World War, including the church, which was rebuilt in a Romano-Byzantine style in the 1920s.

HOUSE OF BRUCE

ROBERT I (1274–1329; r. 1306–1329)

Alexander III having recognised the Bruces as his heirs in default of any surviving issue, the latter accordingly opposed the succession of King John: indeed, they had fought on Edward I's side against him. However, after changing sides a number of times, Robert was finally crowned Scots king on 27 March 1306, but defeated at Methven on 19 June.

Over the next thirteen years, the English were gradually driven out, the war climaxing in the defeat of Edward II at the battle of Bannockburn in 1314. Robert died from a painful skin disease, possibly leprosy, at Cardross Castle, on the Firth of Clyde.

Interment and tomb
After his death, the king's body was brought to Dunfermline and was there buried in the abbey church, in front of the 'new' high altar, in the thirteenth-century eastern extension. The body was placed in a 2.1 metre-long vault, in a double-layered body-form lead coffin, with a linen-and-gold pall. Above the vault was erected a monument made for him in Paris, of gilded marble. Its exact form is uncertain.

Denied the chance to take part in a crusade, the king had directed that his heart be removed and carried to the Holy Land. This was undertaken, but its bearer, Sir James Douglas (1286?–1330), was killed in Spain en route. Brought back to Scotland, it was buried by David II at Melrose Abbey.

Post-interment history
Robert's monument, like most of the furnishings of the abbey, was destroyed at the Reformation. Fragments said to come from it are now in the Museum of Scotland, Edinburgh.

On 17 February 1818, during the reconstruction of the eastern end of the church, a masonry vault was discovered in the centre of the old quire of the abbey, containing a lead coffin, covered by the remains of a decayed pall, incorporating gold thread. The lead was damaged at knees and feet, through which bones could be seen. After this initial discovery, the vault was re-closed

87. Eastern end of Dunfermline Abbey, built in the nineteenth century and covering the tomb of Robert I, who is commemorated around the tower.

88. Leaden coffin of Robert I.

with stones fixed together with iron bars, pending completion of the building work.

On 5 November 1819 the tomb was formally opened. The coffin was found to have further decayed since 1818, several holes now being visible in the lead, through which brownish bones were visible, with much of the pall also having disintegrated. Under the rubbish on the floor of the vault were found

89. Skull of Robert I as revealed in 1819.

the remains of a wooden coffin, apparently of oak, in a damp state. Only a few iron nails were recovered.

To allow access to the burial, the south side of the vault was dismantled and the body and lead covering lifted out. The lead covering was found to be composed of two layers, each about 3 millimetres thick; the outer was in poor condition, but the inner was rather better preserved. The head-end was sawn open to gain access to the skull.

The skull was in perfect condition, but no soft tissues survived anywhere on the body, a fair amount of water being present in the coffin. Some of the upper teeth were missing, with a trace of an old fracture visible on the jaw. The sternum had been sawn through to remove the heart. Although no inscriptions survived (a plate inscribed 'Robertus Scotorum Rex' proving to be a fake), this helped confirm the attribution of the vault, since it tied in with the historic removal of Robert I's heart prior to burial.

After its examination, and the making of a cast of the skull, the skeleton was rewrapped in its lead covering and placed in a new lead coffin, embedded in pitch, into which were placed various books and coins. Having lain a while in state, Robert was re-interred in his vault, which had been rebuilt in brick with an arched roof, enclosed within a stone wall. The new lead coffin had cast on its lid the king's name and dates of his two burials.

While working on the clearance of outer vault, workmen had found a small

90. Cast of the skull of Robert I (Marischel Museum, Aberdeen).

leaden box, lying 3.5 metres north-east of the eastern end of the outer vault. It contained a substance resembling lime, and an amorphous mass, apparently viscera. Although probably nothing to do with king, it was reburied with him.

A memorial slab was unveiled above the vault on 21 December 1889 by Lady Louisa Bruce, comprising a brass inlaid into a porphyry slab. The latter had been acquired by the 7th Earl of Elgin while Ambassador at Constantinople. It had formed part of the lid of a sarcophagus then outside the Nur-i Osmaniye Mosque there, and reputed to be that of Constantine the Great. The slab was donated by the 9th Earl, who had been a member of the committee responsible for King Robert's memorial: Lady Louise was his sister.

A terracotta reconstruction of the king's head, based on the cast of the skull, was prepared in 1996 by Brian Hill, of Newcastle Dental Hospital, using standard soft-tissue depth measurements. In the course of this it was proved that some isolated teeth, found near the body in 1819 and in the possession of the Earl of Elgin, did not actually belong to the king's jaw. At the same time, Peter Vanezis of Glasgow University produced a computer-generated image on a similar basis: the resulting images were remarkably similar.

91. Raised pulpit above the nineteenth-century brass marking the location of the tomb of Robert I.

In March 1921, work by the Office of Works found beneath the chapter house floor at Melrose a leaden casket containing a heart, assumed to be that of Robert. This was rediscovered in August 1996 during excavations by Historic Scotland, and examined on 3 September 1996. A small hole was drilled into the casket and the interior investigated via a fibre-optic device. The outer casket was then opened, revealing a small conical lead casket, with the engraved copper plaque added in 1921. The inner casket was not opened, and was reburied in the abbey in 1997.

DAVID II (1324–1371; r. 1329–1371)

The son of Robert I, by his tenth birthday David had been driven into exile in France by his brother-in-law, Edward III of England, who had shortly before supported a seizure of the throne by Edward Balliol. David returned in 1341, to be wounded and taken prisoner at the Battle of Neville's Cross in 1346. Ransomed in 1357, he maintained peace with England for the rest of his reign. David died suddenly in 1371 at Edinburgh Castle.

Interment and tomb

David was buried in Holyrood Abbey; the exact site of his tomb is unknown.

92. Destroyed eastern end of Holyrood Abbey, former location of the tombs of David II and James II.

HOUSE OF BALLIOL

EDWARD (d. 1363; r. intermittently 1332–1338)
Son of John, Edward was installed on the throne by Edward III and crowned at Scone. Taking refuge in England in 1334/5, he finally fled in 1338 and formally gave up his claim to the throne to Edward III in 1356, in exchange for a pension. He died childless at Wheatley near Doncaster.

Interment and tomb
It may be assumed that Edward was buried near his place of death, perhaps in the Church of St George, but no data is available.

HOUSE OF STEWART*

ROBERT II (1316–1390; r. 1371–1390)
A grandson of Robert I by his daughter, Marjory, Robert II was the seventh in the line of hereditary royal stewards and founded the Stewart dynasty. Having the previous year handed effective executive power to his sons, Robert died at Dundonald Castle, Ayrshire.

Interment and tomb
The king was buried at Scone Abbey, Perthshire, now largely destroyed.

ROBERT III (*c.* 1337–1406; 1390–1406)
John, Earl of Carrick, eldest son of Robert II, had been physically and mentally maimed by a kick from a horse a little before his accession to the throne as Robert III. He died at Rothesay Castle.

Interment and tomb
Robert was interred at Paisley Abbey, Renfrewshire.

Post-interment history
The original tomb having been destroyed at the Reformation, a new monument was placed in the church by Victoria in 1888.

JAMES I (1394–1437; r. 1406–1437)
On Robert III's death, his son, James, was in English captivity. He was not released until 1424. He was murdered on 20 February 1437, at Perth

*Spelled Stuart after the dynasty's assumption of the English throne.

93. East end of Paisley Abbey; the Victorian memorial to Robert III is on the right.

Dominican Monastery, by conspirators who aimed to make his great-uncle, the Earl of Athol, king.

Interment and tomb

The king had erected a 'magnificent' monument for himself in the church of the Charterhouse of Perth (a Carthusian monastery on the South Inch), his own foundation, and it was here that his body was buried. The heart had previously been removed, to be carried on pilgrimage to the Holy Land. However, it got no further than Rhodes, and returned to Perth in 1443/4. A railing was erected around the tomb and other adornments carried out in 1438–40.

Post-interment history

The Charterhouse was sacked and demolished in 1559 and the royal tombs lost. A marble slab formerly bearing brass plates depicting a man and a woman and now in St John's Church, Perth, has been identified as belonging to the tomb of James I and Queen Joan, but may actually be that of a private sepulchre.

94. St James's Hospital, built on the site of Perth's Charterhouse, the burial place of James I.

JAMES II (1430–1460; r. 1437–1460)

The son of James I, James was killed by the accidental explosion of a cannon during a siege of Roxburgh Castle. This was being carried out in support of Edward, Prince of Wales, and Queen Margaret following the capture of Henry VI.

Interment and tomb

The king was buried in the quire of Holyrood Abbey; the exact location of his burial is now lost.

JAMES III (1452–1488; r. 1460–1488)

This young son of James II required a Regency. He died during a rebellion, being murdered at Milltown, Bannockburn, following the Battle of Sauchieburn. The body was found some days later and carried to Stirling for burial.

Interment and tomb

James was interred at Cambuskenneth Abbey, Stirling, near the high altar.

Post-interment history

The abbey church and the royal tomb were destroyed at the Reformation.

95. Cambuskenneth Abbey. The tomb of James III lies to the right, marked by a Victorian memorial.

96. Site of the Charterhouse of Sheen, where reposed the body of James IV.

During excavations in May 1864, a blue limestone slab was found, which had once borne a brass. Underneath was a large oak coffin containing a skeleton, its feet touching the enclosure of the high altar. Preservation was not good, and much of the skeleton crumbled to dust on exposure. The remaining front of the cranium and the mandible were examined and found to be stained a tawny brown colour, unlike other osseous remains from the site. This was attributed to the decay of the coffin.

The remains were re-interred under a new table-tomb.

JAMES IV (1473–1513; r. 1488–1513)
James IV succeeded his father, James III. His reign saw an encouragement of trade and education, but also a renewal of the alliance with France. This led to an invasion of England, during which the king was killed in battle at Flodden Field, Northumberland.

Interment and tomb
James's body was embalmed and encoffined by the victorious Henry VIII, and placed in the Charterhouse monastery at Sheen (Richmond), founded by Henry V in 1414–15.

Post-interment history

The body was disturbed at the time of the Dissolution, and the head hacked from the trunk. The head was described as having 'a sweet savour', and 'dried of all moisture, and yet the form remaining, with the hair of the head, and beard red'. Ultimately the head was buried in the Church of St Michael, on the west side of Wood Street, City of London, near the south side of Gresham Street and along north side of Huggin Lane. The church was first built in 1272–73, with additions made down to 1449. Repaired and remodelled by Sir Christopher Wren in 1675, it was demolished under the Union of Benifices Act 1897. No head was found in deep excavations made during the demolition.

JAMES V (1512–1542; r. 1513–1542)

Only a year old on the death of his father, James began to rule in person in 1524. He died at Falkland soon after hearing of the defeat of his forces in battle with rebellious barons on 15 December 1542.

Interment and tomb

James was apparently interred in the quire of Holyrood Abbey.

Post-interment history

The quire of the church was wrecked by the English in 1544. James's body is reported to have been re-embalmed and moved to a new vault in the south-east corner of the nave during the reign of James VI.

The vault was accidentally found in January 1683 and the contents examined. James's body lay in leaden and wooden coffins, his flesh black, and with hair still on his head. However, five years later, the coffin was opened during the 'purging' of the church by a protestant mob, and left thus. It was seen in this state in 1735, but the lead coffin was stolen in 1768 following the collapse of the church roof, the king's bones being heaped up with those of the other occupants of the vault.

In the mid 1840s the bones were collected together in a single large coffin on the top shelf of the rebuilt vault.

MARY I 'QUEEN OF SCOTS' (1542–1587; r. 1542–1567)

The daughter of James V, Mary went to France as the fiancée of the future François II in 1548, returning on his premature death in 1560. Following the debacle of her further marriages to Lord Darnley and the Earl of Bothwell, she was forced to abdicate in 1567. Mary fled to England, where she was

97. Nave of Holyrood Abbey; the royal vault in which James V was (re?)buried is in the far (south-east) corner.

98. Tomb of Mary, Queen of Scots, in Westminster Abbey; in the foreground is the tomb of Margaret, Countess of Lennox.

imprisoned; becoming implicated in plots against Elizabeth I, she was ultimately executed at Fotheringay Castle on 8 February 1587.

Interment and tomb
The queen was interred at Peterborough Cathedral on 30 July 1587, in a brick grave near the south door of the quire. The location remains marked by a plain black marble slab.

Post-interment history
In 1606 Mary's body was removed to Westminster by James VI & I, and placed in a large vault in the south aisle of Henry VII's Chapel. Above it was erected a monument that was a more elaborate version of that also provided by James for Elizabeth I, costing £825 10s. It was not completed until 1612.

Mary's vault, nearly 4 metres long by 2.75 metres broad and 2 metres high, was later used for the interment of many of her descendants, down to the reign of Anne. When entered by Dean Stanley in 1868, the chamber presented a 'startling, may it almost be said, awful, scene'. Mary's coffin lay below the later case of Arbella Stewart, and was saturated with pitch.

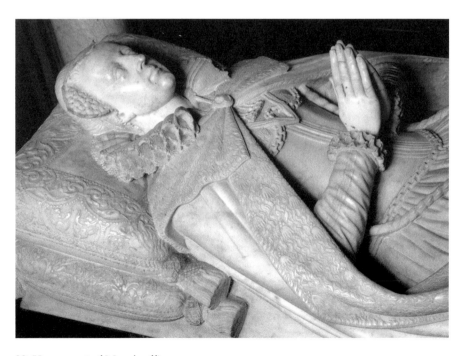

99. Upper part of Mary's effigy.

For James VI, Charles I, Charles II, James VII, William II, Mary II, and Anne, see Part II: England.

For 'James VIII', 'Charles III' and 'Henry I', see Appendix 2.

The thrones of Scotland and England were formally united in 1707.

IV

United Kingdom

HOUSE OF HANOVER

GEORGE I (1660–1727; r. 1714–1727)
King George I was the great-grandson of James VI & I, and succeeded as the senior Protestant member of the royal line. He spent half the year in Hanover, and died of a stroke at Osnabrück on 11 June 1727.

Interment and tomb
King George was buried on 4 Aug 1727 in the crypt of the chapel within the Leineschloss, the city residence of the rulers of Hanover.

Post-interment history
The Leineschloss was badly damaged by bombing during the Second World

100. The Leineschloss, in the crypt of whose chapel George I was originally buried. The building was badly damaged by bombing during the Second World War, and is now the Lower Saxon Parliament.

101. Mausoleum of King Ernst August in the Herrenhausen Gardens at Hanover, where George I was reburied in 1957. In the foreground are the graves of Ernst August, Duke of Brunswick (1887-1953), grandson of Georg V, last King of Hanover, and his wife, Viktoria Luise (1892-1980).

War. In 1957 the royal burials were moved to a mausoleum in the gardens of the former Herrenhausen Palace, the Leineschloss being rebuilt as the Lower Saxon Parliament. The mausoleum had been built for Ernst August, King of Hanover 1837–1851, a younger brother of William IV. Also reburied in 1957 were Duke Johann Friedrich (1625–1679), Elector Ernst August (1629–1690), his wife Sophia (1630–1716, the heiress who brought the British crown to Hanover) and Queen Friederike (1778–1841).

GEORGE II (1683–1760; r. 1727–1760)
The son of George I, his reign saw the establishment of cabinet government, the last Jacobite rebellion and the beginning of a long series of wars against France. George was the last king to lead an army in battle, at Dettingen in 1743. He died of a heart attack at Kensington Palace on 25 October 1760.

Interment and tomb
Work on a royal vault under the central portion of the Henry VII Chapel at Westminster was begun directly after the death of George II's wife, Caroline, on 20 November 1737. Work was commissioned three days later, and a plan

102. Model of the vault of George II.

103. While no Georgian monarch possessed a sepulchral monument, Charlotte, Princess of Wales, daughter and heir of George IV, has this touching monument in St George's Chapel, Windsor. It shows the ascension of the princess and the baby at whose birth she died; their draped bodies lie below.

provided by Henry Flitcroft the next morning(!); construction involved removing the floor of the chapel, making a deep excavation, and constructing a stone complex of some considerable size. Even so, it was ready in time for the Queen's burial in December, three weeks after her death.

A black marble double sarcophagus at the eastern end housed the bodies of the king and queen; white marble sceptres were inlaid into the lid, while leather-covered visceral boxes lay on either side. Lateral chambers were provided for members of the royal family. After George's funeral, the inner side-boards of his and Queen Caroline's coffins were removed to increase their proximity in death.

George was the last British king to undergo the 'traditional' embalming process, he and the queen both being equipped with visceral chests.

Post-interment history

Members of the royal family continued to be interred in the vault until Henry Fredrick, Duke of Cumberland, was laid to rest in 1790. Subsequent openings included those in 1871, and in 1943 by Dean Labilliere, at which time the contents were found to be in good condition, with 'scarcely any signs of decay'.

GEORGE III (1738–1820; r. 1760–1820)

George III was George II's grandson. The latter part of his reign was marred by the loss of the American colonies, and by attacks of porphyria. The latter left him incapable of reigning, Prince George (IV) becoming Regent in 1810. The king died at Windsor on 29 January 1820.

Interment and tomb

George III had a new vault constructed under what is now the Albert Chapel at Windsor, but which had on occasion been intended as the tomb of Henry VII, Cardinal Wolsey and Henry VIII. George's coffin was placed in a niche at the east end of the vault, along with those of members of his family. Unlike his predecessors, the king was not embalmed, being merely wrapped in a waxed cereloth.

Post-interment history

At the end of the nineteenth century the king's coffin was removed from its niche (which was converted into an altar) and placed on the top shelf of Bay 2, on the south side of the vault (see pp. 206-7).

104. Closure of the shaft leading down to the entrance passage of the George III vault at Windsor. It was equipped with a manual lift in Victorian times.

105. The royal vault at Windsor as it was in 1873.

GEORGE IV (1762–1830; r. 1820–1830)

The eldest son of George III, George was an unpopular figure, but a great patron of the arts. He died at Windsor Castle on 26 June 1830.

Interment and tomb

The king's coffin was placed at the eastern end of the eastern bench in the centre of the George III vault at Windsor.

Post-interment history

At the end of the nineteenth century the king's coffin was removed from its bench (which was demolished) and placed on the middle shelf of Bay 2, on the south side of the vault (see pp. 206-7).

WILLIAM IV (1765–1837; r. 1830–1837)

A younger brother of George IV, William had been a professional sailor. His reign saw the passage of the Reform Act of 1832. He died at Windsor Castle on 20 June 1837.

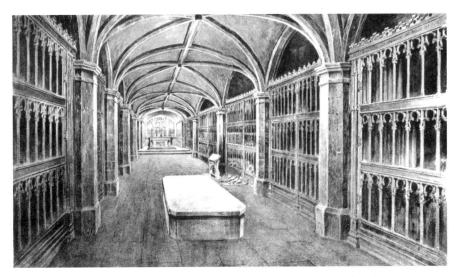

106. The vault as it was in 1910, following major reconstruction a decade beforehand.

Interment and tomb
The king's coffin was placed at the western end of the eastern bench in the centre of the George III vault at Windsor.

Post-interment history
At the end of the nineteenth century the king's coffin was removed from its bench and placed on the bottom shelf of Bay 2, on the south side of the vault (see pp. 206-7).

VICTORIA (1819–1901; r. 1837–1901)
Victoria was a niece of William IV by his brother, Edward, Duke of Kent. Her long reign saw the high point of the British Empire. She was proclaimed Empress of India in 1876. After the longest reign in British history she died at Osborne House, Isle of Wight, on 22 January 1901.

Interment and tomb
Victoria had ordered the construction of a mausoleum at Frogmore in Windsor Great Park within four days of the death of her husband, Albert, Prince Consort, in December 1861, to serve as their joint sepulchre. Construction began in March 1862, and although it was consecrated that December 1862, final completion was only attained in August 1871. The queen's mother, the Duchess of Kent, had previously erected her own mausoleum in the same area.

107. Entrance to the Victoria's mausoleum at Frogmore.

Victoria and Albert's mausoleum was designed by Ludwig Grüner of Dresden, who had previously designed that of Albert's father, Duke Ernst I of Coburg (d. 1844). The architect was Albert Jenkins Humbert and George Dines was the builder. Romanesque in style, the mausoleum is shaped as a Greek cross and has an external diameter of 64 metres, with the external walls built of granite and Portland stone. The interior decoration includes inlays of coloured marbles from around the world and paintings and sculptures in a style imitating Raphael.

In the centre was a double sarcophagus, made from a single piece of grey Aberdeen granite, with marble effigies of the prince and queen sculpted by Baron Carlo Marochetti during 1862–67. Only the former was installed at that time, the queen's being bricked up in a store-room at Windsor, and located at the time of her funeral only through the recollections of an old workman. The reversion to this mediaeval tomb-type seems to have been heavily influenced by recent French practice, and was to be followed by Victoria's two immediate successors.

A crypt was provided under the mausoleum with nine spaces for the queen's children, but none was ever occupied.

HOUSE OF SAXE-COBURG-GOTHA/WINDSOR

EDWARD VII (1841–1910; r. 1901–1910)
Edward was the eldest son of Victoria. His foreign visits proved to be of considerable diplomatic importance. He died at Buckingham Palace on 6 May 1910.

Interment and tomb
Edward VII was provisionally buried at Windsor in the royal vault under the Albert Chapel, on the pedestal just inside the entrance. However, a tomb was completed in 1920 by his wife, Alexandra, at the south side of the high altar in St George's Chapel, directly opposite Edward IV's, and just east of Henry VI's. It bears recumbent marble effigies of the king and queen on a black and green marble sarcophagus (2.36 x 1.70 x 1.02 metres), ornamented with brass. The king's effigy, completed by Bertram Mackennal in 1919, has his favourite dog, Caesar, at his feet.

On the queen's death in November 1925, the king's coffin was removed from the vault and lay with his wife's in front of the altar of the Albert Chapel until 22 April 1927, when both were placed in the sarcophagus, covered with their standards. The monument was formally unveiled on 13 October 1927.

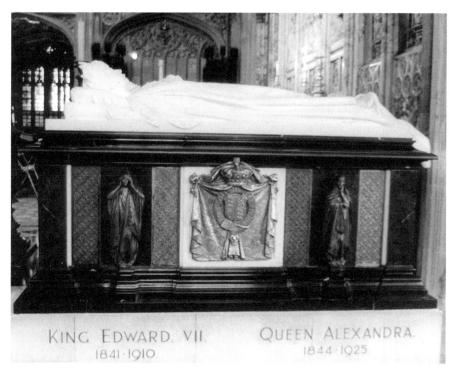

108, 109. Tomb of Edward VII and Queen Alexandra, St George's Chapel, Windsor.

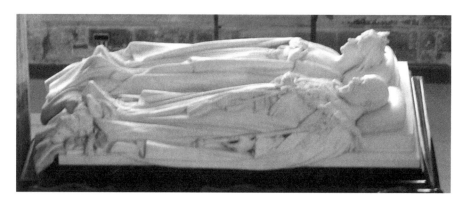

GEORGE V (1865–1936; r. 1910–1936)

George V was Edward VII's second son. His reign saw the passage of the 1911 Parliament Act, the First World War (during which he was injured in a fall from his horse), the partition of Ireland, and the Great Depression. He died at Sandringham House, Norfolk, on 20 January 1936.

110. North-west corner of St George's Chapel, with on the right the tomb of George V. Princess Charlotte's monument (see p. 139) lies in the left-hand corner.

111. Tomb of George V and Queen Mary.

Interment and tomb

The king was initially interred in the royal vault at Windsor. A tomb design was subsequently prepared by Sir Edwin Lutyens (1869–1944) and accepted by the Dean and Canons of Windsor in October 1938. Placed at the west end

112. Graves of the Duke and Duchess of Windsor at Frogmore.

of the north aisle of the nave of St George's Chapel, the tomb comprises a sarcophagus (2.54 x 1.78 x 0.84 metres), decorated with the arms of the king and his wife, Mary, and of the British Dominions and Colonies. It is surmounted by recumbent effigies of the king and queen, carved in *bianca del mare* stone by Sir William Reid Dick (1878–1961). The monument was dedicated on 23 April 1939.

EDWARD VIII (1894–1972; r. 1936)
The eldest son of George V, Edward VIII cut his reign short when he abdicated to marry an American divorcée, Wallis Simpson. After spending much of the remainder of his life in French exile as the Duke of Windsor, the ex-king died of throat cancer in Bois de Boulogne, Paris, on 28 May 1972.

Interment and tomb
Edward's body was returned to the UK and interred in the Royal Burial Ground, Frogmore.

GEORGE VI (1895–1952; r. 1936–1952)
The younger brother of Edward VIII, George VI reigned during the momentous events of the Second World War and its aftermath. Having lost a lung to cancer, the king died in his sleep at Sandringham on 6 February 1952.

113. Chapel of George VI, built onto the north side of St George's Chapel, Windsor.

Interment and tomb

Like his predecessors, George VI was temporarily buried in the George III vault. After considerable discussion, a memorial chapel was constructed for him on the north side of St George's Chapel, the first substantive addition to the structure since 1504. It was designed by George Pace (1915–1975), with the aid of Paul Paget, and constructed by the building firm of Mowlem between 1967 and 1969. The king's coffin was privately transferred to the chapel in March 1969, when the chapel was dedicated by Elizabeth II and Elizabeth, The Queen Mother.

The chapel is entered via a four-centred arch, with a wrought-iron screen and gates, leading into the mortuary chapel itself, beyond which is a small 'liturgical chapel', with an altar. A bronze copy of a medallion of the king, by Sir William Reid Dick, was placed on the back wall of the mortuary chapel. A small vault was constructed below the mortuary chapel, closed with a black ledger-stone simply bearing the king's name.

Post-interment history

The vault was opened on 9 April 2002 for the burial of George VI's widow, Elizabeth. At the same time, the ashes of their daughter, Margaret, Countess

114. Interior of the George VI chapel; the cameo of Queen Elizabeth was made to match that of her husband after her death in 2002.

of Snowdon, who had died that February, were moved there from their temporary resting place in the George III vault. When replaced, the ledger stone additionally bore the king's dates, together with the name and dates of his wife. A medallion to match that of the king was made by Michael Rizzello and unveiled in January 2004.

Appendix 1

The Known Tombs of Royal Consorts

England

Frytheswyda, fl. 665. *Spouse*: Didan of Mercia. *Tomb*: Winchester.
Mother of St Frytheswyda; bones moved to a mortuary chest in the cathedral around 1158, but now lost.

Bertha, d. before 616. *Spouse*: Æthelbert I. *Tomb*: Canterbury, St Augustine's.
Originally buried in the Porticus of St Martin in SS Peter & Paul's Church; later reburied in the abbey church.

Egilfu, d. 944. *Spouse*: Edmund I. *Tomb*: Shaftesbury Abbey.
The abbey and tomb were destroyed at the Dissolution.

Emma, Ælgifu, d. 1052. *Spouses*: Æthelred II; Cnut. *Tomb*: Winchester Old Minster.
Bones moved to the Cathedral; see pp. 200-1.

Edith, d. 1075. *Spouse*: Edward the Confessor. *Tomb*: Westminster Abbey.
Apparently reburied on the left side of the shrine as a result of Henry III's rebuilding of the abbey.

Matilda of Flanders, d. 1083. *Spouse*: William I. *Tomb*: La Trinité, Caen.
The tomb was desecrated in 1562, and the remains moved to a new monument in 1702. The latter was destroyed in 1793, the bones being re-interred below the original grave slab in 1819; they were re-examined in 1961.

Matilda (Maud; Mahalde; Mold) of Scotland, 1080–1118. *Spouse*: Henry I. *Tomb*: Winchester Cathedral (?).
Remains stated to have been placed in a mortuary chest with those of Queen Frytheswyda around 1158; now lost. Another tradition has her buried at Westminster, initially at the entrance of the Chapter House, and then reburied to the south of the Confessor's shrine by Henry III.

Adela of Louvain, d. 1151. *Spouse*: Henry I. *Tomb*: Reading Abbey.
Tomb destroyed at the Dissolution.

Matilda of Boulogne, 1103–1152. *Spouse*: Stephen. *Tomb*: Faversham.
Tomb destroyed at the Dissolution.

Geoffrey V of Anjou, 1113–1150. *Spouse*: Mathilda. *Tomb*: St. Julien's Cathedral, Le Mans, France.

115. The Abbey of La Trinité at Caen, built by Matilda of Flanders, and housing her tomb.

Eleanor of Aquitaine, 1122–1204. *Spouse*: Henry II. *Tomb*: Fontevraud.
Tomb moved on more than one occasion, suffering the same fates as those of Henry II and Richard I. An effigy survives in the abbey.

Berengaria of Navarre, *c.* 1163–1230. *Spouse*: Richard I. *Tomb*: Abbey of L'Epau, near Le Mans, France.
The queen was first buried in the Chapter House, where the skeleton seems to have remained, and was rediscovered in 1960. However, the effigy was apparently shifted after a fire in 1362, and definitively moved to the abbey itself in 1602. It was transferred to the quire on 27 May 1672, where it remained until the French Revolution.

The abbey became a barn, and by 1816 the tomb had been dismantled. It was given to the cathedral of St Julien at Le Mans in 1821, and placed in the north transept. It was subsequently moved within the cathedral in 1860 and

116. The royal effigies at Fontevraud. The nearer pair are those of Queens Eleanor of Aquitaine (*left*) and Isabella of Angoulême.

1921, and then returned to the restored L'Epau Abbey in 1984. Finally, it was placed back in the Chapter House in 1988.

Isabella of Gloucester, *c.* 1175–1217. *Spouse*: John. *Tomb*: Canterbury Cathedral.

No surviving monument.

Isabella of Angoulême, d. 1246. *Spouse*: John. *Tomb*: Fontevraud.

The body was originally buried in the nuns' cemetery, but reinterred in the abbey church in 1254; a wooden effigy there is believed to be hers, suffering the same fates as those of Henry II and Richard I.

Eleanor of Provence, 1217/22–1291. *Spouse*: Henry III. *Tomb*: Amesbury Abbey Church (body); Franciscan Church, London (heart).

Eleanor had become a nun at Amesbury on 7 July 1284. Body: location of burial lost at the Dissolution. Heart: lost after 1547.

Eleanor of Castille, d. 1290. *Spouse*: Edward I. *Tomb*: Westminster Abbey (body); Lincoln Cathedral (viscera); Blackfriars Monastery (heart).

The monument at Lincoln was destroyed during the Civil War, but a replacement was erected in 1891, its effigy a cast of that on her Westminster tomb – which had originally been made as a companion piece. Blackfriars Monastery was destroyed at the Dissolution.

117. The eastern end of the Confessor's Chapel at Westminster; the tomb of Eleanor of Castille, wife of Edward I, is just to the left of Henry V's chantry.

Margaret of France, d. 1317. *Spouse*: Edward I. *Tomb*: Grey Friars' Church, Newgate.
Tomb dismantled 1547; the church was destroyed by fire in 1666; Wren's Christ Church now occupies the site of the six eastern bays.

Isabella of France, 1292–1358. *Spouse*: Edward II. *Tomb*: Grey Friars' Church, Newgate (body); Castle Rising, Lincolnshire (heart).
For Grey Friars' see previous entry. Castle Rising: a slab in the parish church bears the queen's name.

Philippa of Hainault, 1314–1369. *Spouse*: Edward III. *Tomb*: Westminster Abbey.

Anne of Bohemia, d. 1394. *Spouse*: Richard II. *Tomb*: Westminster Abbey.
Buried in the same tomb as her husband.

Isabel of Valois, 1389–1410. *Spouse*: Richard II. *Tomb*: St Laumer Abbey, Blois.
Reburied in Paris, *c*. 1624.

Mary de Bohun, d. 1394. *Spouse*: Henry IV (as Duke of Lancaster and Hereford). *Tomb*: Canterbury Cathedral.
No extant monument.

Joan of Navarre, d. 1437. *Spouse*: Henry IV. *Tomb*: Canterbury Cathedral.
Buried with her husband; the burial was briefly examined in 1832 (see pp. 73-4).

Catherine of Valois, 1401–1437. *Spouse*: Henry V. *Tomb*: Westminster Abbey.
Initially buried in front of the altar of the lady chapel. Her body was wrapped in a sheet of lead and placed in a box alongside the tomb of her husband after the demolition of the Lady Chapel to make way for that of Henry VII. The body was on occasion shown to visitors until buried within the Villiers vault in the St Nicholas Chapel in 1778. By then the upper part of the body, originally well preserved, had been largely destroyed, in part by recent schoolboy vandalism. Finally, on November 1878, now further badly damaged by damp, it was reinterred under a new altar-tomb in Henry V's Chantry.

Margaret of Anjou, 1430–1482. *Spouse*: Henry VI. *Tomb*: Cathedral Church of St Maurice, Angers, France.

Elizabeth Woodville, 1437–1492. *Spouse*: Edward IV. *Tomb*: St George's Chapel, Windsor.
The queen's broken pine coffin and scattered bones were uncovered in the upper part of her husband's vault in 1789.

118. The altar in Henry V's chantry, under which Catharine of Valois was finally reburied in 1778.

Anne Neville, 1456–1485. *Spouse*: Richard III. *Tomb*: Westminster Abbey.
Buried on the south side of altar of the Confessor's Shrine; her leaden coffin may have been one uncovered in 1866.

Elizabeth of York, 1465–1503. *Spouse*: Henry VII. *Tomb*: Westminster Abbey.
Buried in the same tomb as her husband.

Catherine of Aragon, 1485–1536. *Spouse*: Henry VIII. *Tomb*: Peterborough Cathedral.
The tomb is in the north choir-aisle; it was damaged during the Commonwealth. A new marble slab was added above the old bluestone slab in 1895.

Anne Boleyn, 1507–1536. *Spouse*: Henry VIII. *Tomb*: St Peter ad Vincula, Tower of London.
Anne's probable bones were found in 1876; they had apparently been disordered in 1750 when a burial was made nearby. They were reburied in their original location in 1877.

Jane Seymour, *c.* 1509–1537. *Spouse*: Henry VIII. *Tomb*: St George's Chapel, Windsor.
Buried in the same vault as her husband.

Catherine Howard, d. 1542. *Spouse*: Henry VIII. *Tomb*: St Peter ad Vincula, Tower of London.
An attempt to locate her bones in 1876 was unsuccessful.

Anne of Cleves, 1515–1557. *Spouse*: Henry VIII. *Tomb*: Westminster Abbey.
Buried on the south side of altar of the Confessor's Shrine; the tomb was not completed until the reign of James VI & I.

Catherine Parr, 1512–1548. *Spouse*: Henry VIII. *Tomb*: St Mary's Church, Sudeley Castle.
The tomb had been destroyed, and the church become ruinous, by the eighteenth century. The coffin was uncovered and the lead over the face and breast opened in May 1782; the body was found to be well preserved, but further rough exhumations over the three decades reduced it to a skeleton. The coffin was buried in the church's new Chandos vault in 1817 by the Duchess of Buckingham and Chandos. The church was restored down to 1862; a new table tomb and effigy were provided for the queen in 1854.

Lord Guilford Dudley, d. 1554. *Spouse*: Jane. *Tomb*: St Peter ad Vincula, Tower of London.
Probably placed next to his wife, near the north wall of the chancel.

Felipe II of Spain, 1527–1598. *Spouse*: Mary I. *Tomb*: Real Monasterio de San Lorenzo de El Escorial, Spain.

The Monastery was built by the king himself; he is interred in the Royal Pantheon.

Anne of Denmark, 1574–1619. *Spouse*: James VI & I. *Tomb*: Westminster Abbey.

Buried in vault in chapel in north-east corner of Henry VII's Chapel. It appears to have been opened in 1718, and perhaps in 1811; on one of these occasions, all wood was removed, leaving a simple leaden anthropoid shell. It was examined by Dean Stanley in 1868.

Henrietta Maria of France, 1609–1669. *Spouse*: Charles I. *Tomb*: Basilica of St Denis, Paris (body); Convent of Visitandine Nuns, Chaillot (heart).

The burial of the body was desecrated in 1793; the bones are now contained in an ossuary in the crypt of the basilica along with those of the other individuals formerly buried there. The convent building was destroyed during the French Revolution.

Elizabeth Bourchier, 1598–1665. *Spouse*: Oliver Cromwell. *Tomb*: St Andrew's Church, Northborough, Northants.

Dorothy Maijor, 1625–1675. *Spouse*: Richard Cromwell. *Tomb*: All Saints' Church, Hursley. See pp. 102, 104-5.

Catherine of Braganza, 1638–1705. *Spouse*: Charles II. *Tomb*: Monastery of the Hieronymites (Mosteiro dos Jerónimos), Bélem, Lisbon, Portugal.

The monastery was damaged by an earthquake in 1755, after which the tomb was moved from the chancel to the south transept. The body was transferred to the new royal vault in the Church of São Vicente De Fora, Lisbon, in 1855.

Anne Hyde, 1637–1671. *Spouse*: James VII & II (while Duke of York). *Tomb*: Westminster Abbey.

Buried in the vault of Mary, Queen of Scots.

Mary of Modena, 1658–1718. *Spouse*: James VII & II. *Tomb*: Convent of the Visitandine Nuns, Chaillot, France.

Body lost in the French Revolution; coffin plate now in the British Museum (accession number 1878, 11-1.115).

George of Denmark, 1653–1708. *Spouse*: Anne. *Tomb*: Westminster Abbey
Buried alongside his wife.

Scotland

Margaret Atheling, d. 1093. *Spouse*: Malcolm III. *Tomb*: Dunfermline Abbey
Margaret was interred in the original western part of the church. Following her canonisation, the queen's bones were moved to a silver reliquary at the eastern end of the extension added to the church around 1250. The shrine

was destroyed in 1560. Some of the postcranial bones are were acquired by Felipe II of Spain, and placed in two urns in the church of San Lorenzo in the Escorial. In the nineteenth century an attempt was made to repatriate these remains, but they could not be found. The head of the queen was allegedly hidden by a Benedictine monk in Fife and then taken to Antwerp. In about 1627 it was translated to the Scots College at Douai and there exposed to public veneration. It was still to be seen there in 1785; it was well preserved and had very fine fair hair. It disappeared during the French Revolution.

Sybilla of England, d. 1120. *Spouse*: Alexander I. *Tomb*: Dunfermline Abbey.
Interred in the original western part of the church.

Matilda of Huntingdon, d. 1130/31. *Spouse*: David I. *Tomb*: Scone Abbey.
The abbey was destroyed at the Reformation.

Ermengarde de Bellomonte, d. 1233. *Spouse*: William 'the Lion'. *Tomb*: Balmerino Abbey, Fife.
The abbey was destroyed at the Reformation.

Joan of England, d. 1237. Spouse: Alexander II. Tomb: Nunnery Church, Tarrant Crawford, Dorset.
The church was demolished after 1539; no trace of the queen's tomb survives.

Margaret of England, d. 1274. *Spouse*: Alexander III. *Tomb*: Dunfermline Abbey.
Interred in the original western part of the church.

Elizabeth de Burgh, d. 1327. *Spouse*: Robert I. *Tomb*: Dunfermline Abbey.
Interred in the eastern extension of the church. Hers may have been the vault found near the king's in 1917–18, containing a female skeleton with long reddish hair. It was reburied by the Earl of Elgin in a new vault under the south transept.

Euphemia Ross, d. 1387. *Spouse*: Robert II. *Tomb*: Paisley Abbey.
The tomb was destroyed in the 1560s.

Annabella Drummond, d. 1401. *Spouse*: Robert III. *Tomb*: Dunfermline Abbey.
Interred in the eastern extension of the church.

Joan Beaufort, d. 1445. *Spouse*: James I. *Tomb*: Charterhouse, Perth.
Totally destroyed; see p. 129.

Mary of Gueldres, d. 1463. *Spouse*: James II. *Tomb*: Trinity Church, Edinburgh.
Her presumed remains were reburied in the royal vault at Holyrood following demolition of Trinity Church in 1848. A second set of remains, also potentially hers, were later buried just outside the vault.

Margaret of Denmark, *c*. 1457–1486. *Spouse*: James III. *Tomb*: Cambuskenneth Abbey.

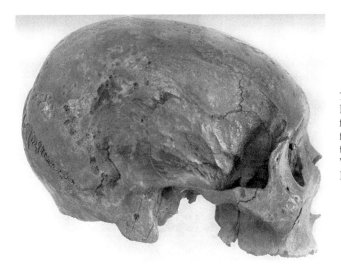

119. The skull of Lord Darnley, looted from his tomb, and finally destroyed in the Second World War bombing of London.

Buried in the same tomb as her husband (pp. 130-1).

Margaret Tudor, 1489–1541. *Spouse*: James IV. *Tomb*: St John's, Perth.

Madeleine de Valois, d. 1538. *Spouse*: James V. *Tomb*: Holyrood Abbey.
The burial was desecrated in 1688 and 1768, her skull (and perhaps a femur) being stolen on the second occasion. Her remains are now mixed with those of other occupants of the vault in the same coffin (see p. 132).

Mary of Guise, 1515–1560. *Spouse*: James V. *Tomb*: Reims Cathedral, France.

François II of France, 1544–1560. *Spouse*: Mary. *Tomb*: St Denis, Paris.
The burial was desecrated in 1793; the bones now contained in an ossuary in the crypt of the basilica, along with those of the other individuals formerly buried there.

Henry Stewart, Lord Darnley, 1545–1567. *Spouse*: Mary. *Tomb*: Holyrood Abbey.
The burial was desecrated in 1688 and 1768, Darnley's skull and a femur being stolen on the second occasion. The skull was acquired by the Royal College of Surgeons, London, in 1869, together with a femur (perhaps of Madeleine de Valois); a second femur alleged to be Darnley's was acquired in 1880. All these bones were destroyed in the bombing of the college in 1941. Darnley's other remains are now mixed with those of other occupants of the vault in the same coffin (see p. 132).

James Hepburn, Earl of Bothwell, c. 1536–1578. *Spouse*: Mary. *Tomb*: Fårevejle Church, Denmark.
Traditionally thought to lie in a vault in a side-chapel, the plain wooden coffin alleged to be his was opened on 30 May 1858 and the body examined. The head was well preserved but had apparently been separated from the

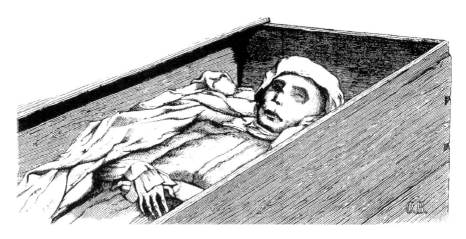

120. The body of the Earl of Bothwell, last consort of Mary, Queen of Scots, as revealed in 1858.

trunk by an earlier examination. The coffin was then moved to a vault in the chancel of the church.

Great Britain

Sophia Dorothea of Brunswick-Lüneburg and Celle, 1666–1726. *Spouse*: George I. *Tomb*: Stadtkirche, Celle.

Caroline of Brandenburg-Anspach, 1683–1737. *Spouse*: George II. *Tomb*: Westminster Abbey.
Buried in same sarcophagus as her husband in his vault.

Charlotte of Mecklenburg-Strelitz, 1744–1818. *Spouse*: George III. *Tomb*: St George's Chapel, Windsor.
Interred in the royal vault.

Caroline of Brunswick, 1768–1821. *Spouse*: George IV. *Tomb*: Brunswick, Germany.
Buried alongside her father, Duke Karl II of Brunswick-Wolfenbüttel.

Adelaide of Saxe-Meiningen, 1792–1849. *Spouse*: William IV. *Tomb*: St George's Chapel, Windsor.
Interred in the royal vault.

Albert of Saxe-Coburg Gotha, 1819–1861. *Spouse*: Victoria. *Tomb*: Royal Mausoleum, Frogmore.
Buried in the same tomb as his wife.

Alexandra of Denmark, 1844–1925. *Spouse*: Edward VII. *Tomb*: St George's Chapel, Windsor.

Buried in same tomb as her husband.

Mary of Teck, 1867-1953. *Spouse*: George V. *Tomb*: St George's Chapel, Windsor.

Buried in the same tomb as her husband.

Elizabeth Bowes-Lyon, 1900–2002. *Spouse*: George VI. *Tomb*: St George's Chapel, Windsor.

Buried in the vault alongside her husband.

Appendix 2

The Stuarts in Exile

Following the flight of James VII & II in 1688 and the Act of Settlement of 1701, which conferred the succession on the descendants of the Electress Sophia of Hanover, the senior surviving Protestant member of the royal house, the Stuart claim was upheld by the exiled King James, by his son, James 'VIII & III' ('The Old Pretender'), and by the latter's children, Charles 'III' ('The Young Pretender', 'Bonnie Prince Charlie') and Henry 'I & IX'. Abortive attempts at restoration by force were made in 1715 and 1745, leaving the Jacobite (from the Latin form of 'James') pretenders resident in Italy, where Henry entered the Catholic Church as a cardinal. With his death, the male Stuart line became extinct. The tombs of all three 'Kings Across the Water' lie in Italy.

JAMES 'VIII & III', Prince of Wales (1688–1766)
The Old Pretender was buried in the crypt of the Basilica of San Pietro in Vatican City. His tomb was subsequently marked with a slab, proclaiming him 'James III, King of Great Britain, Scotland, France, and Ireland'. A plan to erect a monument in the basilica above, designed by Pietro Bracci (1700–1773), came to nothing.

James's wife, Clementina Sobieska, had been buried in the crypt in 1735, but moved ten years later to the rear of her monument, on the spiral staircase leading to the dome and roof of the basilica.

CHARLES 'III', Count of Albany (1720–1788)
His elder son, however, was interred in the Cathedral of San Pietro at Frascati, where his brother had been Bishop since 1761. It was marked by a white marble monument over 3.5 metres high, surmounted by the royal arms in bronze. Its text calls him the son and heir of James 'III', and proclaims the residual hereditary rights of his brother, Henry. The prince's heart was buried separately in a leaden urn under the pavement in front of the monument.

The body itself was moved to the Vatican in 1807, and was placed alongside that of his father, with a tombstone calling him Charles III.

HENRY 'I & IX', Cardinal Duke of York (1725–1807)

The cardinal's burial took place alongside that of his father in the Vatican, his tomb-stone calling him Henry IX, and listing his various church appointments. At the same time, his brother's body was moved from Frascati to lie with that of Henry.

In 1810, the cardinal's executor commissioned Antonio Canova (1767–1822) to design a monument to be placed in the basilica itself. A number of designs were produced, but it was not until 1815 that sufficient funds were raised, a substantial contribution being made by George, Prince Regent (later George IV). Earlier, Henry, impoverished as a result of the French Republican invasion of Italy, had received a pension from the 'usurping' George III; the irony was now compounded by his son's contribution to a memorial that was to commemorate not just Henry, but all three men who wholly rejected the Hanoverian right to the British throne. In 1819, the white marble monument was finally completed, and installed against the first pier of the left aisle of the basilica.

Upon it are, from the left, relief portraits of James, Henry and Charles, surmounted by the royal arms. Its Latin inscription is interesting in that it gives James his claimed regnal number, but calls him only the son of James II; Charles is simply 'Charles Edward', while Henry is 'Henry, Dean of the Cardinal Fathers'. Clearly, the monument's principal donor had limits to his indulgence of the Stuart claims!

In August 1938, the bodies of the three Stuart 'kings' were moved slightly further east, to make way for the planned tomb of Pope Pius XI (d. 1939). The following year a single travertine sarcophagus, topped by a bronze crown, was erected over the three interments, its inscription mirroring that on the Canova monument. It seems that the cost of the new tomb was met by George VI, continuing the tradition of the third and fourth Georges; the sarcophagus was formally handed over to the Vatican authorities on 20 March 1939, by Cardinal Hinsley, Archbishop of Westminster. The now-surplus tombstones are now on display in the crypt of the chapel of Pontifical Scots College, in the north-west part of Rome.

After the death of Cardinal Henry, the Stuart claim to the throne passed to the descendants of James VII & II's youngest sister, Henrietta Anne. At the time of writing, this rests in the House of Wittelsbach, the former royal house of Bavaria, although the heirs 'neither press nor deny' the claim.

The Stuart 'line of succession' and list of royal burial places is as follows:

Appendix 2

Name	Burial place
Carlo Emanuele IV, King of Sardinia (1751–1819)	Rome: Church of Sant' Andrea al Quirinale
Vittorio Emanuele I, King of Sardinia (1759–1824)	Turin, Italy: Basilica di Superga
Maria Beatrice of Savoy, Duchess of Modena (1792–1840)	Modena, Italy: Church of San Vincenzo
Francesco V, Duke of Modena (1819–1875)	Vienna: Kapuzinerkirche
Maria Theresa of Austria-Este, Queen of Bavaria (1849–1919)	Chapel of Schloss Wildenwart, Germany; moved 1921 to Munich Cathedral
Rupprecht, Crown Prince of Bavaria (1869–1955)	Theatinerkirche, Munich
Albrecht, Duke of Bavaria (1905–1996)	Andechs, Germany: Klosterkirche & Friedhof

Appendix 3

Foreign Monarchs Buried in Great Britain

NAPOLÉON III OF FRANCE (1808–1873; r. 1852–1870)
The nephew of Napoléon I, as Louis-Napoléon Bonaparte, he was elected President of France in 1848. He re-established the Empire following a coup and plebiscite, but abdicated in the wake of France's defeat in the Franco-Prussian War. He then went into exile in England, where he died after an operation at Chislehurst, Kent. He was buried there in St Mary's Catholic Church, where he was joined by his son, the Prince Imperial, after the latter's death, serving with the British Army in South Africa, in 1879. A mortuary chapel was built onto the church specifically to house the remains, a marble slab set into the floor commemorating their burial there.

The bodies were subsequently reburied in St Michael's Abbey at Farnborough, built by Napoléon III's widow, Eugénie, between 1883 and 1888 as the family mausoleum. The abbey church was designed by the French architect Gabriel Destailleur in the late French Gothic style; in the imperial crypt below are three sarcophagi of Scottish granite and gifts from Queen Victoria. That above the main altar belongs to the empress, with those of her husband and son in two side chapels.

GEORG V OF HANOVER (1819–1878; r. 1851–1866)
The Hanoverian and British thrones separated on the accession of Victoria, the Salic law of succession used in Hanover excluding women from the succession. Hanover therefore passed to Victoria's eldest surviving uncle, Ernst August, succeeded in turn by his son Georg, blind from 1833 onwards. The king handled the clash between Austria and Prussia in 1866 badly, with the result that Hanover was invaded by the latter and formally annexed in September 1866.

Georg spent the rest of his life in exile in Austria and France, dying in Paris while visiting the city for medical advice on 12 June 1878. He was buried in St George's Chapel, Windsor, in the royal vault (see pp. 206-7). He is commemorated by a plaque adjacent to the monument of Princess Charlotte in the north-west corner of the chapel.

121. Memorial to an exiled monarch, Georg V of Hanover, in St George's Chapel. His body lies in the royal vault there.

Appendix 4

Principal Chapels, Churches and Mausolea Containing Royal Tombs

ARBROATH, Angus
Abbey Church of the Virgin Mary and St Thomas à Becket
A Benedictine house founded by William the Lion in 1178, the eastern part of the church was sufficiently complete in 1214 to receive the body of its founder; the whole building was completed in 1233. It had a choir of three bays and a nave of nine, with side aisles, two transepts, a central and two western towers. After the Reformation, the lady chapel was used as for protestant worship until 1590, after which the whole church fell into ruin.

BEC, Normandy, France
Abbaye de Bec
This Benedictine foundation came into existence in the early eleventh century, moving twice before the definitive church was begun around 1040. The French Revolution led to the structure being used as a barracks, as it remained from 1792 to 1948. It was then reclaimed by the Benedictines; as the original church was now a ruin, the 1747 refectory became the new abbey church.

BOSHAM, Sussex
Holy Trinity Church
Much of the church is of late tenth-century date. A thirteenth-century crypt lies in the south-east corner of the south aisle, while other changes were made over the centuries.

CAEN, Normandy, France
Abbaye de Saint Etienne
This church was built to fulfil the terms laid down for papal approval of William I's marriage to his distant cousin, Matilda. This required that they should found a monastery and a nunnery, respectively. William's abbey was consecrated in 1077, Matilda's Abbaye de le Trinité in 1066.

Rebuilding of the western end took place in the thirteenth century, but the church was pillaged by Huguenots in 1562, the collapse of the spire in 1566

122. The Abbey of St Etienne at Caen.

leaving it ruinous. Repairs initiated in 1599 were finally completed in 1626, with further restoration from 1710 to 1763. The monks were expelled in 1790, the church reopening as a parish church in 1802.

CAMBUSKENNETH, Stirlingshire
Abbey Church of St Mary
Founded by David I in 1140, the church was destroyed by the Reformers in 1560, only the thirteenth/fourteenth century bell-tower and a few fragments of wall now remaining.

CANTERBURY, Kent
Abbey Church of St Augustine
In 598 St Augustine was granted land by the newly-converted King Æthelbert as the site of a monastery. The first main church was that of SS Peter and Paul, completed around 613. Another church, of St Mary, was built to the east around 620. The former building was extended during the tenth century, the two churches being united by a probably never-finished rotunda in the 1150s. The Saxon structures were replaced by a new building during the late eleventh and early twelfth centuries.

The abbey was surrendered to the crown in 1538, parts of the monastery

123. The bell-tower – the sole standing remnant of Cambuskenneth Abbey.

124. The ruins of St Augustine's Abbey at Canterbury; the cathedral can be seen in the background.

125. Canterbury Cathedral.

becoming a royal palace. However, the church was dismantled from 1541, only those parts that had formed part of the palace surviving to any substantial degree.

Cathedral of Christ Church
The cathedral originated in Saxon times. Complete rebuilding was begun in 1070. Although finished seven years later, it was later considerably enlarged in the early twelfth century, only to be gutted by fire in 1174. Reconstructed once again, the cathedral was greatly enriched by the shrine of St Thomas Becket (d. 1170), and had a new nave and transepts built during the late fourteenth century. A new lady chapel followed the next century, with the central tower replaced around 1500. The last major structural change came in the 1830s, when the north-west tower was replaced.

CHERTSEY, Surrey
Abbey Church of St Peter
The Benedictine Chertsey Abbey was founded in 666 by King Ecgbriht I of Kent, and re-founded by Edgar in 964. The abbey and monastery were rebuilt

126. The eastern part of Canterbury Cathedral. The shrine of St Thomas Becket lay behind the high altar, beyond the top of the steps; it was flanked on the left by the tomb of Henry IV, and on the right by that of the Black Prince.

in 1110, and approximated to Westminster Abbey in size, but suffered dissolution on 6 July 1537. Stone from the abbey was used by Henry VIII to construct Oatlands Palace near Weybridge, only a few fragments of stonework and paving now surviving in the abbey gardens.

DUNFERMLINE, Fife
Abbey Church of the Holy Trinity

Dunfermline Abbey was begun by Queen (St) Margaret in 1072 and was completed and the building dedicated to the Holy Trinity two years later; its foundations were discovered in 1916. It was in two parts, with a nave and tower to the west and a subsequently-added quire and apse. A complete reconstruction was completed and the new building consecrated in 1150. A number of kings from Duncan II to Malcolm IV were buried here in front of the main altar. A new quire was added to the east to accommodate the

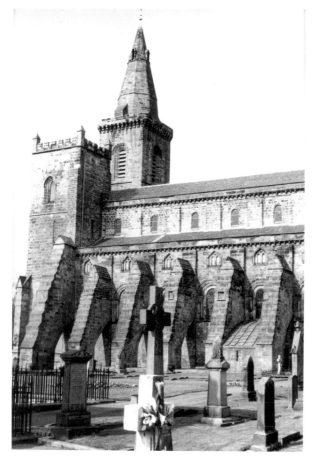

127. The surviving
mediaeval portion of
Dunfermline Abbey.

foundress's shrine the following century, and in front of its altar were laid to rest both Alexander III and Robert I. The north porch of the nave was added in 1450. On 29 March 1560 the chancel of the church was destroyed along with the monastic buildings, but the central tower and the nave, which acted as a parish church, were left intact.

The walls were buttressed in 1620 and 1625, but in 1753 the central tower fell down. Then, in 1807, the south-east tower was struck by lightning and collapsed. After rejecting a completely fresh site to the south, it was decided in 1817 that a new church should be built onto the truncated eastern end of the abbey church. It thus occupied part of the area once occupied by the quire, although leaving the foundations of St Margaret's shrine beyond the end.

EDINBURGH
Abbey of Holyrood
Holyrood was founded by David I in 1128, with major rebuilding taking place from the thirteenth century onwards. James V spent considerable sums on its repair and enlargement, but in 1547 the monastic buildings, as well as the

128. The palace of Holyroodhouse and the ruins of the Abbey of Holyrood.

129. The royal vault, showing the upper portion added in 1844.

choir, lady chapel, and transepts of the church were destroyed by Edward Seymour, Earl of Hertford (later Duke of Somerset), leaving only the nave in a serviceable state. Twenty years later, the interior was sacked by a mob of John Knox's supporters. Some of the royal burials formerly in the quire were subsequently moved to a new vault in the south-east corner of the nave by James VI. On the northern side was laid James V, to the south of him being Lord Darnley; east of them was the Countess of Argyll (illegitimate daughter of James V, d. 1557), and against the south wall Queen Madeleine de Valois. Two of her infant children lay next to her.

A new east window was inserted for Charles I's coronation in 1633, and after the Restoration the church became a chapel royal for Charles II. Made into the chapel of the Order of the Thistle by James VII & II, it was sacked by a mob in 1688, when the royal lead coffins were sold for their metal, but the bodies left in place, where they were seen in 1735. They were again disturbed in 1768, following the collapse of the church roof, and the skulls of Queen Madeleine and Darnley stolen. Seen piled in a heap in 1844, all the bones from the vault were then put together in one coffin and put on an upper shelf in the vault. The presumed remains of Mary of Gueldres (wife of James II) were reburied there in 1848.

FAVERSHAM, Kent
Abbey Church of Our Saviour
A Benedictine monastery of the Cluniac Congregation, Faversham Abbey was founded in 1147 by Stephen. Its grants and privileges were confirmed by Henry II, John and Henry III, although its annual grant was cancelled in 1209. This led to the plan being changed in 1220, the western arm being finished some 5.5 metres short, and the incomplete eastern one cut back by 26 metres, leaving just the royal chapel. Work was finally finished around 1251.

The abbey was dissolved in 1538 and subsequently demolished. Much of the building material was used to strengthen English fortifications in Calais, and by the end of the seventeenth century all visible traces had disappeared. The church was excavated in 1964, in advance of building work on the site.

FONTEVRAUD (Fontévrault), France
Abbaye de Fontevraud
The abbey at Fontevraud was founded in the early twelfth century and consecrated in 1119. Following the burial of Henry II there, royal links were strongly maintained, a number of royal ladies retiring there, including Queen Eleanor of Aquitaine.

As a result of the Revolution, the last monks and nuns were expelled in 1792. After lying derelict, the abbey became a prison in 1804, remaining so until 1962. The church was restored during 1902–10, while a systematic programme of excavation and restoration began in 1965–70.

GLASTONBURY
Glastonbury Abbey
The first stone abbey church at Glastonbury was founded by King Ina in 712. It was lengthened by St Dunstan, who also added the Cloisters in 940. The old church was demolished and replaced by a larger structure in 1077, in turn replaced by a yet bigger church in 1118. The subsidiary buildings were renewed in 1125. Unfortunately, the whole abbey was destroyed by fire in 1184. When reconstructed, the site of the old church was marked by the new lady chapel, which lay at the west end of the new Great Church, consecrated in 1213, and completed in 1291. The quire of the Great Church was extended

130. Fontevraud Abbey.

131. The interior of Fontevraud Abbey, showing the present (and probably approximate original) location of the royal tombs.

132. View of the ruins of Glastonbury Abbey. In the foreground is the lady chapel, built on the site of the church burnt down in 1189.

by two bays in 1348 and the cloisters rebuilt in 1415. The abbey was dissolved in 1539 and the structure sacked. In 1908 the abbey ruins were purchased by the Bath and Wells Diocesan Trust and consolidation and repair begun.

GLOUCESTER
Cathedral Church of St Peter
The origins of Gloucester Cathedral go back to a monastic foundation of Osric of Mercia in 681. A new abbey church was begun in 1089, dedicated in 1100, and completed around 1126. Rebuilding took place in the first half of the thirteenth century, including a new tower, and again from 1331, following the burial of Edward II. The tower was renewed again in the 1450s, and the lady chapel added in 1470.

The church became a cathedral following the Dissolution. Major restoration work was carried out in the seventeenth, eighteenth and nineteenth centuries.

Saint Oswald's Priory Church
The church (originally St Peter's) was constructed from the blocks of a nearby Roman temple in the 890s. An elaborate eastern crypt was added in the tenth/eleventh century. The church was repaired and enlarged down to the thirteenth century, and after the dissolution of the priory in 1537, the north

133. The west end of Gloucester Cathedral.

134. The eastern part of Gloucester Cathedral; Edward II's tomb lies on the centre-left.

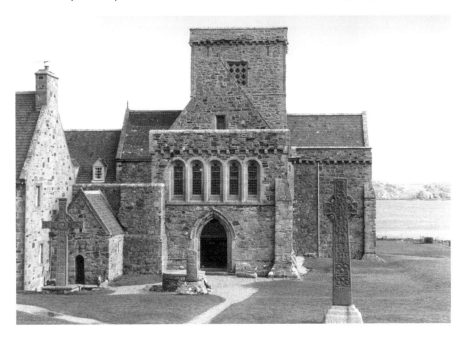

135. The Abbey of Iona.

aisle of the church became the parish church of St Catherine in 1548. However, it had fallen into disrepair by 1643, when it may have also been damaged during the Civil War. It began to be dismantled in 1654, and was largely demolished in 1656, being reduced to its foundations, save part of the northern arcade of the nave.

IONA
According to tradition, the earliest Scottish royal burials took place in the 'Reilig Odhráin' ([St] Oran's Burial Ground) on Iona. The chapel there, restored in 1956, is generally regarded as the earliest standing monument. Forty-eight kings of Scotland, beginning with Fergus, and four of Ireland are reputed to have been buried there. No certain trace of the tombs has ever been found, the extant tomb-slabs probably belonging to West Highland chieftains.

KING'S LANGLEY, Hertfordshire
Priory Church of the House of the Friars Preachers
This Dominican foundation was built adjacent to the royal palace in King's Langley during 1308–12, the church being consecrated in 1312. Apart from Richard II's original burial, other significant interments included Piers Gaveston, the favourite of Edward II, in 1315 and Edmund of Langley, Duke

179

of York, son of Edward III, in 1402. The tomb of Edmund was removed to the local parish church at the time of the Dissolution.

LEICESTER
Abbey Church of St Mary
Leicester's Franciscan ('Grey Friars') Abbey was founded in 1132 by Robert le Bossu, Earl of Leicester, and consecrated in 1143. Dissolved in 1538, the whole establishment has now almost entirely disappeared and is built over by later streets and buildings.

LONDON
St Paul's Cathedral
The first wooden church on the site was erected in 604 by Æthelbert I of Kent. It was destroyed by fire and rebuilt in 675–85, but sacked by the Danes in 962. A new church was then burnt in 1087. A massive new structure was constructed between then and 1240, a new quire being completed in 1313.

The cathedral was sacked in 1549 by a mob and gradually fell into disrepair. Renovation work was begun by Inigo Jones in a classical style, most notably with an incongruous new west front, but terminated in 1642 by the Civil War, which saw further damage. In 1660 Christopher Wren was commissioned to undertake major repairs to the building, but soon afterwards it was badly damaged in the Great Fire of 1666.

Temporary repairs were made, but it was soon decided that a wholly new building was required. Demolition began in 1668, and the new structure, designed by Wren, was finished in 1710, although available for services since 1697.

Tower of London, Chapel of St Peter ad Vincula
The Chapel of St Peter ad Vincula was founded prior to the reign of John – probably under Henry I. Modifications were made under Henry III, but the structure was entirely rebuilt by Edward I. A fire in 1512 caused damage, and major alterations were then made on the orders of Henry VIII. Various more minor modifications were undertaken in subsequent reigns, until a substantial restoration in 1876–77. During the work on the chapel pavement, a number of burials were examined.

MALMESBURY
Abbey Church of SS Peter, Paul, Aldhelm and Mary
A monastery was first established on the site in around 676. A new church was consecrated in about 1180. Over the next two centuries the building was

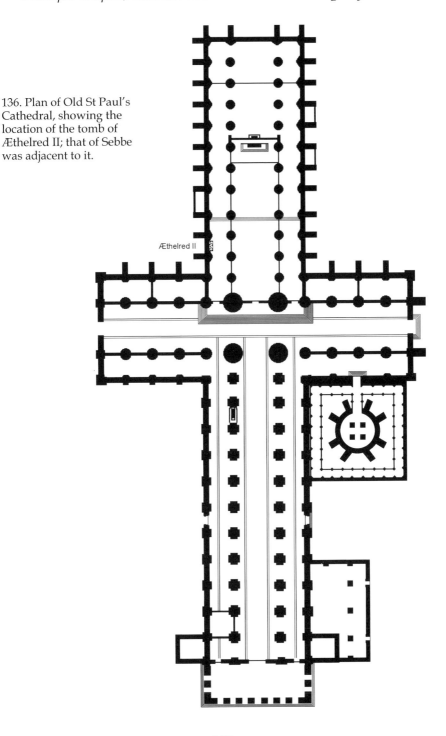

136. Plan of Old St Paul's Cathedral, showing the location of the tomb of Æthelred II; that of Sebbe was adjacent to it.

Æthelred II

137. Malmesbury Abbey.

enlarged, including the addition of a very tall spire which, however, fell down around 1500. The monastery was dissolved in 1539, but the abbey church was bought by William Stumpe, who arranged for its consecration as the parish church in 1541. The west tower collapsed around 1600, and had largely fallen out of use by the eighteenth century. The crossing and western arm of the church are almost entirely destroyed, the current church being restricted to the original nave.

Major restoration took place in 1928, and the church was from 1928 to 1995 the seat of a suffragan bishop.

MELROSE, Roxburghshire
Abbey Church

Founded by David I in 1136, the church was rebuilt in the fifteenth century. A further extension to the west was stopped suddenly after the Scottish defeat at Flodden in 1542. The abbey was burned three times, in 1322 by Edward II, in 1385 by Richard II, and finally in 1545 by the Earl of Hertford. The monks' quire was restored in the seventeenth century as a church, but ultimately fell into disuse.

PAISLEY, Renfrewshire
Abbey Church

The abbey at Paisley was founded by Walter the Steward in 1163, but burned by the English in 1307. It was subsequently rebuilt, but burned again in the

138. The ruins of Melrose Abbey.

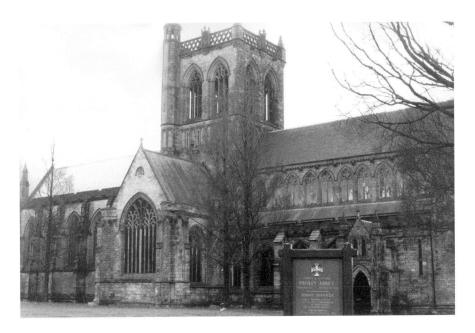

139. Paisley Abbey.

fifteenth century. Following another reconstruction, the tower collapsed and wrecked the quire in the 1560s, leaving only the nave. This was walled off to become the parish church for the reformed church.

Some restoration was carried out in the 1770s, another programme beginning in 1862. Major reconstruction was carried out from 1898 to 1907, when the transepts were brought back into use. Finally between 1917 and 1928, the tower was re-erected, together with the quire and cloisters.

PERTH, Perthshire
Charterhouse of the Carthusians

The charter for this monastery was granted by James I in December 1429, with building work beginning the following year. Its church seems to have been intended as James's burial place, and he was interred there in 1437, as was Queen Joan Beaufort. Queen Margaret Tudor was also buried there in 1541. However, on 11 May 1559, John Knox preached at Perth, as a result of which a mob sacked and demolished the Charterhouse. Its site is now occupied by the Hospital of James VI, although geophysical survey there in 1995 was inconclusive.

READING, Berkshire
Abbey Church of Virgin Mary and St John the Evangelist

Reading Abbey was founded by Henry I in 1121 and was finished in 1164, some 137 metres long; a lady chapel was added to the east end in 1314. Following the Dissolution, the church fell into ruin, only some of the walls of the transepts and parts of the foundations now surviving.

REPTON, Derbyshire
Church of St Wystan

The church was founded in the eighth century, and although rebuilt in the thirteenth and fifteenth centuries, parts of the chancel and nave may be original. A crypt constructed as a royal burial place around 750 also still survives; it has a vaulted ceiling in nine bays supported on round arches. The crypt appears to have been converted into a shrine for pilgrims after the burial there of St Wystan in 850.

ROUEN, France
Cathedral of Notre Dame des Pres

The origins of this church go back to the fourth century, remains being excavated during 1985–95. A new structure was completed by Henry I in 1063, with major rebuilding being undertaken in the thirteenth century, and more

140. St Wystan's Church, Repton, Mercia's royal mausoleum.

141. St Wystan's Church: the royal vault lies below the Saxon east end of the building.

142. Rouen Cathedral.

substantial work during the following two centuries, the south tower being built during the fifteenth. The cathedral was essentially completed with a new gothic façade at the beginning of the sixteenth century.

Severe damage was suffered during the siege of Rouen in 1592, but rebuilding was completed in 1604. Further reconstruction in 1734 resulted in the destruction of a number of early monuments, including those of Richard I's heart, Henry 'the Young King' (1155–1183), John, Duke of Bedford (1389–1435), and the heart of Charles V of France (1364–1380).

SHAFTESBURY
Abbey Church of St Mary and St Edward

The institution was founded by Ælfred around 888, his daughter becoming the first abbess. It became a centre of pilgrimage following the burial there of Edward the Martyr, and became the largest and richest Benedictine house for women in England.

Within ten years of the Dissolution in 1539 the church began to fall into disrepair, and was gradually quarried away. The ruins passed through various hands, until in 1930 ownership was taken by Mrs Frances Claridge. In 1951, the abbey was purchased by Laura Sydenham and Phyllis Carter, from whom in January 1986 the Shaftesbury Abbey and Museum Preservation Trust obtained the site.

SHERBORNE
Abbey Church of St Mary the Virgin

The church was a cathedral from 705 to 1075, a Benedictine monastery from 998 to 1539, and then the local parish church. It became the seat of a suffragan bishop in 1925. It was rebuilt in the twelfth and fifteenth centuries. At the Dissolution, the church was bought by Sir John Horsey who resold it as the town's new parish church. From 1848 onwards there has been an almost continuous process of repair, consolidation and restoration.

TYNEMOUTH
Priory Church of the Blessed Virgin and St Oswin

The Saxon Priory of Tynemouth grew up around the grave of St Oswin in the churchyard of St Mary. It was, however, plundered repeatedly by the Danes and by 1008 had been abandoned. The institution was refounded under Edward the Confessor, the saint's relics being rediscovered 1065. Owing to delays in completing the new church, however, they were translated to Jarrow until 1083.

A large new church was completed by Robert de Mowbray, Earl of

143. Sherborne Abbey.

Northumberland, around 1090. A lady chapel was added in the fourteenth century, but the church fell into ruin following the Dissolution.

WESTMINSTER
Collegiate Church of St Peter

The date of the foundation of the abbey is uncertain. Tradition ascribes it to Saeberht, King of Essex, in 616, but the earliest evidence dates to the eighth century. A new church was begun by Edward the Confessor in 1055 and consecrated in 1065. However, in 1245 all but the nave was demolished by Henry III, to construct the present building. Rebuilding of the old nave was begun around 1376, and work on the church continued until 1517. The last major element of this work was the replacement of the lady chapel with the chapel of Henry VII, begun in 1502.

The monastery was dissolved in 1539, and the following year the church became the cathedral of the new see of Westminster, suppressed a decade later. In 1556 Westminster regained monastic status under Mary I, but the monks were definitively expelled in 1559. The following year, the church was refounded by Elizabeth I as a collegiate church and royal peculiar. No further building took place until the eighteenth century, when the western towers were added, to the design of Nicholas Hawksmoor and John James; they were completed in 1745. Internal

144. Westminster Abbey, the principal burial place of English kings.

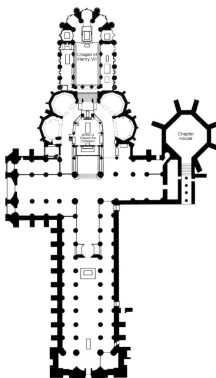

145. Plan of Westminster Abbey.

146. Edward the Confessor's Chapel in Westminster Abbey.

restoration was carried out in the nineteenth century, including a remodelling of the area of the high altar by Sir George Gilbert Scott in 1867.

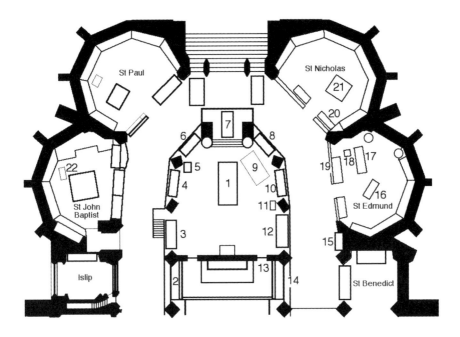

147. Plan of the Confessor's Chapel (royal and related tombs only).

1. **Edward the Confessor**.
2. Edmund, Earl of Lancaster (1296; son of Henry III).
3. **Edward I**.
4. **Henry III**.
5. Elizabeth (1495; daughter of Henry VII).
6. Eleanor of Castille (wife of Edward I).
7. **Henry V**.
8. Philippa of Hainault (wife of Edward III).
9. Thomas, Duke of of Gloucester (1397; son of Edward III).
10. **Edward III**.
11. Margaret (1472; daughter of Edward IV).
12. **Richard II** and Anne of Bohemia.
13. Anne Neville (wife of Richard III).
14. **Saebehrt**.
15. Katharine (1257; daughter of Henry III); Richard (son of Henry III); John (son of Henry III); John (son of Edward I); Alfonso (1284; son of Edward I); Henry

(son of Edward I); Eleanor (daughter of Edward I).
16. Eleanor, Duchess of Gloucester (1399; daughter-in-law of Edward III).
17. Frances, Duchess of Suffolk (1559; mother of Jane).
18. William of Windsor (1348; son of Edward III); Blanche of the Tower (1342; daughter of Edward III).
19. John, Earl of Cornwall (1336; son of Edward II).
20. Philippa, Duchess of York (1431; granddaughter-in-law of Edward III).
21. Sir George and Mary Villiers (1605 and 1632; vault later used for second reburial of Catharine of Valois).
22. Hugh and Mary de Bohun (1304 and 1305; grandchildren of Edward I; first placed at 12; before being moved to St Nicholas' Chapel and finally to that of St John the Baptist).

191

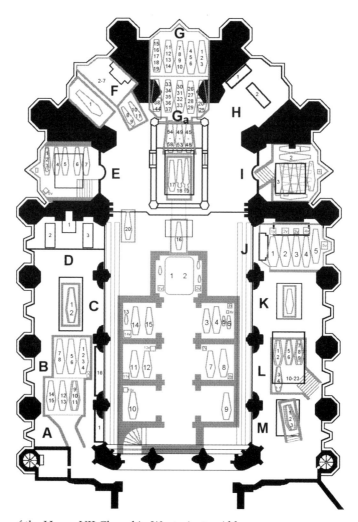

148. Plan of the Henry VII Chapel in Westminster Abbey.

1. George II.
2. Caroline (1737; wife of George II).
3. Louisa Anne (1751; daughter of George II).
4. Edward Augustus, Duke of York (son of George II).
5. Still-born child of George II.
6. George (son of George II).
7. Amelia (1786; daughter of George II).
8. Caroline Elizabeth (1757; daughter of George II).
9. Henry Frederick, Duke of Cumberland (son of Frederick, Prince of Wales, 1790).
10. William Augustus, Duke of Cumberland (1765; son of George II).
11. Elizabeth Caroline (1759; daughter of Frederick, Prince of Wales).
12. Frederick William (son of Frederick, Prince of Wales).
13. Alfred (son of George II).
14. Frederick Lewis, Prince of Wales (1751; son of George II).
15. Augusta, Princess of Wales (1772).
16. Edward VI.
17. James VI & I.
18. Elizabeth of York (wife of Henry VII).
19. Henry VII.
20. Elizabeth Claypole (1658; daughter of Oliver Cromwell).

A.1. Monument of Charles Montague, Earl of Halifax (1715).

B. Vault of General Monck: **B.1.** George Monck, Duke of Albemarle (1670); **B.2.** Duchess of Albemarle (1670); **B.3.** Joseph Addison (1719); **B.4.** James Craggs (1720); **B.5.** George Fitzroy, Duke of Northumberland (1716); **B.7.** Elizabeth, Lady Stanhope (1708); **B.8.** Charles Montagu, Earl of Halifax (1715); **B.10.** Frances, Lady Carteret (1743); **B.11.** John, Earl Granville (1763); **B.12.** Mary, Duchess of Northumberland (1738); **B.13.** Grace, Countess Granville (1744); **B.14.** Elizabeth, Duchess of Albemarle (1734); **B.15.** Sophia, Countess of Granville (1745); **B.16.** Monument of George Saville, Marquess of Halifax (1695).

C. Monument of Elizabeth I: C.1. **Elizabeth I**; C.2. **Mary I**.

D.1. '**Edward V**' and 'Richard, Duke of York'; **D.2.** Sophia (1606; daughter of James VI & I); **D.3.** Mary (1607; daughter of James VI & I).

E. Monument of the Duke of Buckingham: **E.1.** Lord Francis Villiers (1648); **E.2.** George Villiers, Duke of Buckingham (1628); **E.3.** George Villiers, Duke of Buckingham (1687); **E.4.** Mary, Duchess of Buckingham (1704); **E.5.** Charles Hamilton, Earl of Selkirk (1738); **E.6.** Catherine, Viscountess Grandison (1725); **E.7.** General William Steuart (1726).

F. Monument of the Dukes of Buckinghamshire: **F.1.** Anne of Denmark (wife of James VI & I); **F.2.** John Sheffield, Duke of Buckinghamshire (1721); **F.3.** Catharine, Duchess of Buckinghamshire (1743; illegitimate daughter of James VII & II); **F.4.** Edmund, Duke of Buckinghamshire (1735); **F.5-7.** Two sons and a daughter of F.2 & 3 (transferred from St Margaret's, Westminster, 1721); **F.8.** Archibald Campbell, Duke of Argyll (1761); **F.9.** Caroline Campbell, Countess of Dalkeith (1791); **F.10.** Duchess of Argyll (1767); **F.11.** Mary Coke, Viscountess Coke (1811).

G. RAF Memorial Chapel, with vault made for Oliver Cromwell. Buried in the chapel are Hugh, Viscount Trenchard (1956) and Hugh, Baron Dowding (1970); **Ga.** Extension made to vault for James Butler, Duke of Ormonde (1688): burials include children of the Duke of Monmouth and Charles Fitzcharles, Earl of Plymouth (1680; illegitimate son of Charles II).

H.1. Antony, Duc de Montpensier (1807;

brother of Louis Philippe of France); **H.2.** Arthur Penrhyn Stanley (1881; Dean of Westminster) and Lady Augusta Stanley.

I. Monument of the Dukes of Richmond: **I.1.** Esme Stuart, Duke of Richmond (1660); **I.2.** Catharine, Duchess of Abercorn (1723); **I.3.** Mary, Countess of Kildare (1683); **I.4.** Heart of Esme Stuart (see M.1 – interred 1661); 20+ other coffins of members of Lennox family, including: Ludovic Stuart, Duke of Richmond (1624); Elizabeth, Duchess of Richmond (1661); John, Earl of Kildare (1707); Charles Lennox, Duke of Richmond (1723; illegitimate son of Charles II).

J. Monument of George Monck, Duke of Albemarle: **J.1. Anne**; **J.2.** George of Denmark (husband of Anne); **J.3. William III**; **J.4. Mary II**; **J.5. Charles II**.

K. Monument of Margaret Beaufort (1509; mother of Henry VII).

L. Monument of **Mary** (of Scots): **L.1. Mary** (of Scots); **L.2.** Arbella Stuart (1615); **L.3.** Henry, Prince of Wales (1612; son of James VI & I); **L.4.** Henry, Duke of Gloucester (1660; son of Charles I); **L.5.** Rupert, Duke of Cumberland (1682; son of Elizabeth of Bohemia); **L.6.** William, Duke of Gloucester (1700; son of Anne); **L.7.** Mary of Orange (1660; mother of William III); **L.8.** Elizabeth of Bohemia (1662; daughter of Charles I); **L.9.** Anne Hyde, Duchess of York (1671; wife of James VII & II); **L.10.** Charles, Duke of Cambridge (1661; son of James VII & II); **L.11.** James, Duke of Cambridge (1667; son of James VII & II); **L.12.** Charles, Duke of Kendale (1677; son of James VII & II); **L.13.** Edgar, Duke of Richmond (1671; son of James VII & II); **L.14.** Charles, D. of Cambridge (1677; son of James VII & II); **L.15.** Henrietta (1669; daughter of James VII & II); **L.16.** Katharine (1671; daughter of James VII & II); **L.17.** Katharine Laura (1675; daughter of James VII & II); **L.18.** Isabella (1680; daughter of James VII & II); **L.19.** Anna Sophia (1686; daughter of Anne); **L.20.** Mary (1686; daughter of Anne); **L.21.** Mary (daughter of Anne); **L.22.** George (son of Anne); **L.23.** James Darnley (1686; illegitimate son of James VII & II).

M. Monument of Margaret, Countess of Lennox: **M.1.** Esme Stuart, Duke of Richmond (1624); **M.2.** Charles, Earl of Lennox; **M.3.** Margaret, Countess of Lennox (1578; grandmother of James VI & I).

149. The east end of Westminster Abbey, with Henry VII's Chapel in the foreground. The difference between the structures' architectural styles is very evident.

150. Interior of Henry VII's Chapel.

WHITBY
Abbey Church
Whitby Abbey was founded in 657 by the abbess Hild, with resources given to her by King Oswiu in celebration of his victory over Penda of Mercia. It became a major seat of learning, but was sacked by the Danes in 867. Whitby was not re-founded until around 1067; major rebuilding took place in the thirteenth and fourteenth centuries. Following the onset of the Black Death in 1349, the monastery began its decline, and was finally suppressed in December 1539. The nave collapsed in 1762, followed by the central tower and west front later in the century. The ruins were excavated in the 1920s.

WIMBORNE MINSTER, Dorset
Collegiate Church of St Cuthburga
Dedicated to the sister of Ina, the church was founded around 705, but destroyed by the Danes under Æthelred II. It was rebuilt during 1120–80, and became a royal peculiar in 1318. In 1846 the royal peculiar was abolished, and extensive restoration took place during 1855–57.

151. Wimborne Minster.

152. Winchester Cathedral.

WINCHESTER
Priory Church of St Peter (later St Swithun) 'Old Minster'

The history of the great churches of Winchester is a complex one. The city was the original capital of Wessex and so England, many kings from the first conversion to Christianity being buried there. What later came to be called the 'Old Minster' was begun in the seventh century, being dedicated by King Cenewalh who was buried in the vicinity of its high altar in 674.

The tenth century saw the translation into the church of the bones of St Swithun, who had been bishop from 852 to 865, together with those of other Saxon saints. These acts were accompanied by major alterations to the structure of the church, which continued to be the burial place of many of the kings of Wessex and England. Their bodies were concentrated around the high altar and, perhaps, after the translation of St Swithun in 971, around his grave as well. It is possible that earlier royal burials were moved to this latter area.

Following the Norman Conquest, an entirely new church, the present cathedral, was begun in 1079; it lay directly adjacent to the older structure, whose site it ultimately partly overbuilt. In 1093, the monks and the shrine of St Swithun moved into the first phase of new structure, and the demolition of the Old Minster was initiated.

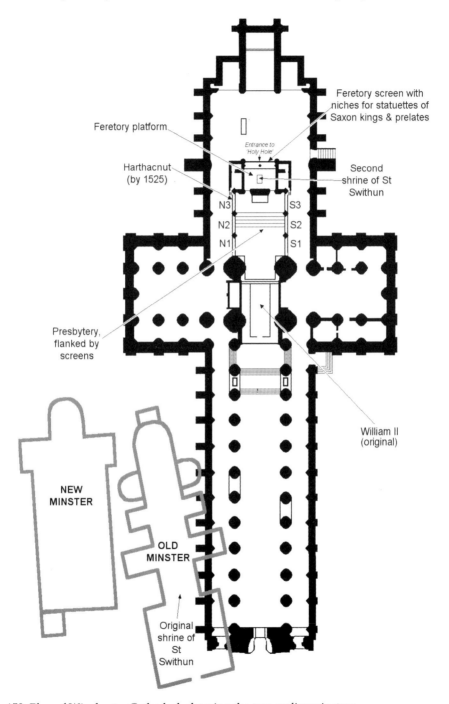

Feretory screen with niches for statuettes of Saxon kings & prelates

Feretory platform

Entrance to 'Holy Hole'

Harthacnut (by 1525)

Second shrine of St Swithun

N3 S3

N2 S2

N1 S1

Presbytery, flanked by screens

William II (original)

NEW MINSTER

OLD MINSTER

Original shrine of St Swithun

153. Plan of Winchester Cathedral, showing the two earlier minsters.

'New Minster'
A second major church was founded directly north of the Old Minster by King Ælfred, although possibly not actually begun until after his death. It was completed around 903, Ælfred being reburied there; it also became the sepulchre of Edward the Elder and his family.

The church was short-lived, losing its importance after the building of the cathedral and the enlargement of the nearby royal palace. Finally, Henry I ordered the transfer of the whole establishment to Hyde, a kilometre north of its old site; the New Minster was then demolished after 1110.

Hyde Abbey
The new abbey was occupied from 1110; the royal tombs were also moved and installed in front of the high altar in 1112. Parts were rebuilt in the late twelfth/early thirteenth century, but the whole structure was destroyed following the dissolution of the monasteries in 1539. The eastern end of the church is now marked by the Hyde Abbey Garden, opened in June 2003, with the architectural elements marked by paving and plants, with three inscribed ledger stones marking the locations of the royal tombs.

Cathedral Church of the Holy and Undivided Trinity
A brand-new church was begun in 1079 and consecrated in 1093, with the nave completed somewhat later. The tower – below which William II was buried in 1100 – collapsed in 1107, but was subsequently rebuilt. Following a reconstruction and extension of the eastern part of the church around 1200–35, major reconstruction of the western part of the cathedral took place during the second half of the fourteenth century.

It is uncertain exactly when the royal burials in the Old Minster were moved into the new building; they may have lain for over half a century in a 'memorial court' in what had been the western part of the demolished Old Minster, around the former grave of St Swithun, just to the left of the new cathedral's façade, or may have been temporarily placed in the crypt. However, under Bishop Henry of Blois (1129–1171), a raised platform was built behind the high altar of the cathedral, with a tunnel underneath known as the 'holy hole'. The latter seems to have allowed pilgrims to crawl under the shrine of St Swithun which lay on the platform until 1476. In 1158 the royal bodies (and those of certain bishops) which had been in the Old Minster were moved to the cathedral and placed around the saint's platform in lead cases. It appears, however, that precise identification of individuals was not possible, and that the remains were mixed up in their coffers. At least some of the aforementioned lead cases were provided with (replacement?) outer

154. The northern part of the presbytery of Winchester Cathedral, showing the mortuary chests of (*from left*) Cnut, William II, Emma, Wina & Ælfwine; Cynewulf & Egbert; and Cynegils & Æthelwulf.

155. The platform over the 'holy hole' at Winchester. The niches, which currently hold a series of icons, formerly contained statuettes of individuals, including a number who were at one time buried above.

wooden chests during the fifteenth century, bearing the names of the individuals whose bones lay within; the two of the chests which survive today belonged respectively to Egbert & Cynewulf and Cynegils & Æthelwulf. The former chest seems to have lain apart from the others, being 'above the heart-tomb of Nicholas of Ely', in the centre of the south side of the presbytery.

Early in the fourteenth century the apsidal end of the platform above the 'holy hole' was replaced by a straight façade and screen with flanking figures of Jesus and Mary, and sixteen statuettes of Saxon worthies, including kings and prelates whose remains lay beyond: Cynegils; Bishop St Birinus; Cynewulf; Egbert, Æthelwulf; Ælfred; Edward the Elder; Æthelstan; Eadred; Edgar; Queen Emma; Bishop Ælfwine; Æthelred II; Edward the Confessor; Cnut; Harthacnut.

A major rearrangement took place during the first half of the sixteenth century, when a series of screens were erected around the presbytery as part of a scheme initiated by Bishop Richard Fox (1448–1528) after 1501. A stone tomb, with a plaque, was provided for Harthacnut, in the north screen, while the remaining kings, queen and bishops were placed atop the screens with new outermost mortuary chests, apparently made around 1525-30. Here, they were joined by the bones of William II. An account of 1635 states that there were at this time ten chests, apparently attributed as follows:

North	South
1. Queen Emma and 'her son' (= Harthacnut?)	1. Cnut and Harthacnut
2. St Birinus	2. Egbert
3. Bishop Ælfwine	3. Ælfred
4. Bishop Wina	4. Æthelwulf
5. Bishop Stigand	5. Cynegils

However, this list is at least in part erroneous. Ælfred had not been buried in the cathedral at all; Æthelwulf and Cynegils had already been paired up in the sixteenth century; Harthacnut had had his own tomb since at least 1525; and William II's name had been seen on a chest some forty years before.

More confusion was caused on 14 December 1642, when the cathedral was sacked by Parliamentary troops during the Civil War. The chests allegedly containing the remains of William II, Queen Emma, 'Harthacnut' (actually Cnut), 'Edward the Confessor' (true identity uncertain) and the bishops were pulled down and their contents flung around the church. Only four of the chests remained undamaged; new ones were made to match them in 1661. The latter pair were only inscribed – collectively for Cnut, William II, Emma, Wina and Ælfwine – around 1685, with an additional inscription recording the desecration and subsequent restoration. From this point the arrangement of outer chests was as follows, counting from the west:

<table>
<tr><td>*North*</td><td>*South*</td></tr>
</table>

North	*South*
N1. Cnut, William II, Emma, Wina and Ælfwine	S1. Cnut, William II, Emma, Wina and Ælfwine
N2. Cynewulf and Egbert	S2. Edmund (son of Ælfred)
N3. Cynegils and Æthelwulf	S3. Eadred

The bones were left at peace for a century, until three Yorkshire Militia officers opened them in the summer of 1797. The examination was carried out by one Henry Howard of Corby Castle, and Mr Hastings, a military surgeon, and involved all six chests. The contents were catalogued as follows:

N1. Mass of leg and thigh bones; one set belonged to a smaller individual.	S1. Mass of leg and thigh bones.
N2. Remains of two skeletons, plus three skulls, one smaller than the others.	S2. Five skulls and a number of thigh bones.
N3. Two skulls and two sets of leg and thigh bones.	S3. Two skulls and many thigh bones.

Another examination by a local antiquary, Francis Joseph Baigent, took place in 1874, and then in November 1886, George Kitchin, Dean of Winchester (1827–1912), had the two eastern chests opened, to reveal sixteenth-century inner ones. The northern one had texts that agreed with those of the outer chest, but the southern one named the occupants as Egbert and Cynewulf – whose outer chest lay in the centre of the north screen! As for their contents, the northern chest agreed with the 1797 inventory, but the southern one had the post-cranial bones of five persons, but no skulls. Clearly there had been confusion when the bones had been replaced in 1797 or 1874.

The outer chests were repainted and reinscribed in 1864 and 1893, with new inner chests provided in 1932: on this occasion the muddle was added to when the positions of the Eadred and Edmund chests were switched. They were opened once more in 1959 for 'cleaning'; a brief examination in April 1991 gave the following 'head-count':

N1. Cnut, William II, Emma, Wina and Ælfwine	Long bones only.	S1. Cnut, William II, Emma, Wina and Ælfwine	Long bones only.
N2. Cynewulf and Egbert	Three skulls, two very incomplete.	S2. Eadred	Two skulls, plus a fragment.
N3. Cynegils and Æthelwulf	Two skulls.	S3. Edmund	Five skulls.

It has been suggested that the twelfth skull (only eleven names appearing on the chests) might be the one missing from a tomb originally in the presbytery and probably belonging to Bishop Henry of Blois (see p. 52), introduced during the 1661 clear-up.

WINDSOR, Berkshire
The Queen's Free Chapel of St George
The first chapel on the site, dedicated to St Edward the Confessor, was built in 1240 by Henry III. However, its dedication was later superseded by one to St George, as a result of the chapel's association with the Order of the Garter, founded in 1348 by Edward III. A new chapel was begun directly to the west in June 1475, under the auspices of Edward IV, to the designs of Henry Janyns. Edward was buried there in 1483, the bulk of the building being completed the following year. The west front was completed under Henry VII in 1509,

156. Windsor Castle, as seen from Eton. St George's Chapel may be seen at the right-hand extremity of the fortress.

157. St George's Chapel.

158. The quire of St George's Chapel; Henry VIII's vault lies under the slab in the middle. Just in front of the step is the mechanical descent into the passage to the George III vault.

159. The nave of St George's Chapel.

160. Plan of St George's Chapel
and the Albert Chapel.

1. Memorial of Princess Charlotte
   (1817; daughter of George IV).
2. **George V** and Mary of Teck
   (1953).
3. **George VI**, Elizabeth
   Bowes-Lyon (2002) and
   Princess Margaret, Countess of
   Snowdon (2002).
4. **Edward IV** and Elizabeth
   Woodville (1492).
5. George and Mary (1479 and
   1482; children of Edward IV).
6. Lift to the royal vault.
7. Stairway to the royal vault.
8. The royal vault: see fig. 161.
9. Memorial to Albert, Prince
   Consort.
10. Albert Victor, Duke of Clarence
    (1892; son of Edward VII).
11. Leopold, Duke of Albany (1884;
    son of Victoria).
12. **Edward VII** and Alexandra of
    Denmark.
13. **Henry VI**.
15. William, Duke of Gloucester
    (1805; son of George II); Maria,
    Duchess of Gloucester (1807);
    William Frederick, Duke of
    Gloucester (1834); Mary,
    Duchess of Gloucester (1857);
    Sophia Matilda (1844); Caroline
    Augusta Matilda (1775).
16. Memorial of Napoléon, Prince
    Imperial.

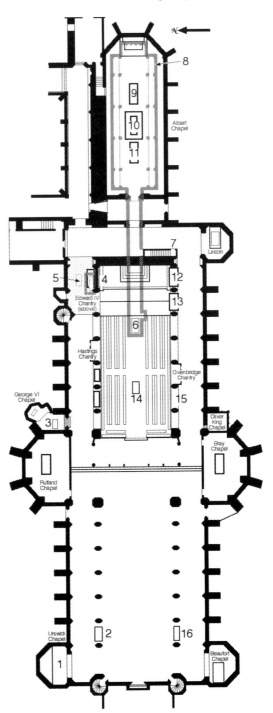

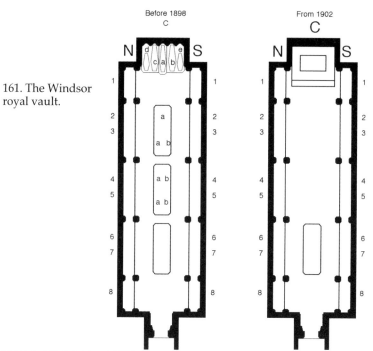

161. The Windsor royal vault.

	1873		1873-1898		1910	
Octavius (1783; son of George III: moved from Westminster).	C1	d	C1	d	S1	b
Alfred (1787; son of George III: moved from Westminster).	C1	e	C1	e	S1	d
Amelia (1810; daughter of George III).	C1	c	C1	c	S1	c
Augusta, Duchess of Brunswick (1813; daughter of George II).	N2	d	N2	d	N2	d
Daughter of the Duke of Cumberland (1817).	N1	b	N1	b	N1	c
Princess Charlotte (1817).	C4	a	N2	c	N2	c
Child of Princess Charlotte (1817).	C4	b	N2	c	N2	c
Heart of Princess Charlotte (1817).	C5	a	N2	c	N2	c
Charlotte (wife of George III).	C1	b	C1	b	S3	b
Edward, Duke of Kent (1820; father of Victoria).	C5	b	N4	c	N3	b
Heart of Duke of Kent.	C5	a	N3	a	N3	a
George III.	C1	a	C1	a	S2	b
Daughter of William IV (1821).	N1	d	N1	d	N1	c
Frederick, Duke of York (1827; son of George III).	N1	c	N1	c	N1	d
George IV.	C2	a	C2	a	S2	c
William IV.	C3	b	C3	b	S2	d
Augusta (1840; daughter of George III.)	N5	d	N5	d	N3	d
Adelaide (wife of William IV).	C3	a	C3	a	S3	d
2 children of Helena (1875 and 1877 – grandchildren of Victoria).					N1	b
Georg V of Hanover (1878).					S4	d
Daughter of Frederica of Hanover (1881).					N2	b
Mary Adelaide, Duchess of Teck (1897).					S4	c
Francis, Duke of Teck (1900).					S5	c

with additional stone vaulting added in 1528. Apart from a number of acts of restoration, in particular by Henry Emlyn in 1785–91, the chapel has remained essentially unchanged until the present day, the only substantive addition being George VI's memorial chapel in the 1960s.

A large vault was built by George III under the adjoining Albert Chapel in 1804, but accessible only from the quire of St George's, where a portion could be raised for lowering coffins into the passage that led into the vault. The latter was arranged with a niche and raised stone platform at one end for its founder and his immediate family at the east end, a series of benches in the centre for later kingly burials, and numerous shelves along the sides for lesser interments. The vault was steadily used during the first half of the nineteenth century; Albert, Prince Consort, and Leopold, Duke of Albany, were temporarily buried in the vault in 1861 and 1884, prior to their respective reburials at Frogmore and in the Albert Chapel.

Alterations were undertaken by Sir Gilbert Scott in 1873, when steps, closed by a slab of stone, were added behind, and to the south of the high altar to aid access to the vault. Further major work was carried out between 1898 and 1902, when George III's dais at the far end was replaced by a sanctuary and altar, the coffins being moved to side shelves. Other coffins previously laid on the benches in the centre aisle were also so-relocated, leaving only a single mortuary table near the entrance. This was to accommodate subsequent arrivals, pending movement to a shelf or tomb elsewhere (cf. pp. 145-6, 148-9). The shelves were now equipped with bronze grilles.

A mechanically-operated platform was also installed in the quire to ease the descent of coffins, electric light fitted, and the stairway added in 1873 opened out, walled and equipped with a gate. Burials continued until 1927, but the following year all coffins subsequent to that of Georg V of Hanover were removed to the Royal Burial Ground at Frogmore. The vault has subsequently been used only for the temporary deposit of interments prior to private burial elsewhere (see pp. 208-9).

The Albert Chapel

All but the north wall of Henry III's original chapel was demolished following 1494 when a new lady chapel – ultimately the Albert Chapel – was begun on its site by Henry VII. This was initially intended for a reburial of Henry VI, and then for the tomb of Henry VII himself. However, neither interment took place, and the chapel was left unfinished at the latter's death. Its structural completion was initiated in 1511, the building then being handed over to Cardinal Thomas Wolsey 1475–1530 as his own 'tomb-house'. On his fall, the

162. The Albert Chapel, begun by Henry VII but not completed for half a millennium.

chapel began to be prepared as Henry VIII's sepulchre, but the tomb was never completed, although Elizabeth I and Charles I apparently subsequently contemplated its use.

Despoiled under the Commonwealth, the tomb-house subsequently narrowly escaped demolition to make way for a tomb of Charles I, and was then equipped as a Roman Catholic chapel of James VII & II in 1686. Following his deposition, it fell derelict once more, and was finally cleared out when the George III vault was excavated through the floor in 1804. The building was finally finished in 1863, when it was fitted out as a memorial to Albert, Prince Consort, adorned with marble and mosaic, with the prince's cenotaph in front of the altar. The final addition was an elaborate monument to Albert Victor, Duke of Clarence (1864–1892), who was transferred from the George III vault below.

The Royal Burial Ground, Frogmore
The area south-west of Queen Victoria's Mausoleum was consecrated in October 1928 to form a cemetery for lesser members of the royal family,

163. The royal burial ground and royal mausoleum at Frogmore.

superseding the George III vault in St George's. At this time, nine coffins were transferred from the old vault, the earliest being that of Prince Francis of Teck, the latest that of Rupert, Viscount Trematon (1907–1928, a great-grandson of Victoria).

Many bodies interred in the Royal Burial Ground have previously rested temporarily in the George III vault after their funerals, before private transfer to Frogmore. The longest such stay was that of George, Duke of Kent (1902–1942), who was not transferred until the death of his wife, Princess Marina, in 1968, to allow their joint interment.

WORCESTER
Cathedral Church of Christ and the Blessed Virgin Mary
A Benedictine monastery was established at Worcester by Bishop Oswald in 983, but partially destroyed in 1041. Rebuilding began in 1084, but was hampered by a fire and the collapse of the central tower around 1202. Nevertheless, work was largely completed by 1218, when the rededication took place. The lady chapel was completed in 1224, and most of the nave was rebuilt in the fourteenth century. The central tower was finished by 1374.

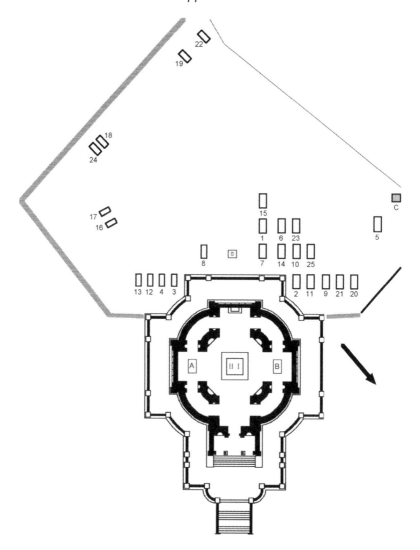

164. Plan of the mausoleum and burial ground at Frogmore
(* = transferred from the royal vault, St George's Chapel).

I. Victoria.
II. Albert, Prince Consort.
 1. Francis of Teck (1910*, brother-in-law of George V).
 2. Louise, Duchess of Connaught (1917*; daughter-in-law of Victoria).
 3. Christian of Schleswig-Holstein (1917*; son-in-law of Victoria).
 4. Helena, Princess Christian of

Schleswig-Holstein (1923*; daughter of Victoria); two infant sons.
 5. Leopold Mountbatten (1922*; grandson of Victoria).
 6. Adolphus, Marquess of Cambridge (1927*; brother-in-law of George V) and Margaret Grosvenor, Marchioness of Cambridge (1929).
 7. Rupert, Viscount Trematon (1928*; great-grandson of Victoria).

8. Victoria (1935; daughter of Edward VII).
9. Arthur of Connaught (1938; grandson of Victoria).
10. Louise, Duchess of Argyll (1939; daughter of Victoria).
11. Arthur, Duke of Connaught (1942; son of Victoria).
12. Helena Victoria of Schleswig-Holstein (1948; granddaughter of Victoria).
13. Marie Louise of Schleswig-Holstein (1956; granddaughter of Victoria).
14. Alexander, Earl of Athlone (1957; brother-in-law of George V) and Princess Alice, Countess of Athlone (1981; granddaughter of Victoria).
15. Marie (1961; wife of King Alexander I of Yugoslavia).
16. George, Duke of Kent (1942; son of George V).
17. Marina of Greece, Duchess of Kent (1972).
18. Edward, Duke of Windsor (1972; **Edward VIII**).
19. Prince William of Gloucester (1972; grandson of George V).

20. Sir Alexander Ramsay (1972; grandson-in-law of Victoria).
21. Lady Patricia Ramsay (1974; granddaughter of Victoria).
22. Henry, Duke of Gloucester (1974; son of George V) and Alice, Duchess of Gloucester (2004).
23. George, Marquess of Cambridge (1981; nephew of George V) and Marchioness of Cambridge (1986).
24. Wallis Warfield, Duchess of Windsor (1986).
25. Sir Henry Abel-Smith (1983; great-grandson-in-law of Victoria) and Lady May Abel-Smith (1994; great-granddaughter of Victoria).
A. Memorial to Edward, Duke of Kent (father of Victoria – moved from St George's Chapel 1950).
B. Memorial to Princess Alice, Grand Duchess of Hesse (1878; daughter of Victoria).
C. Memorial to Prince Maurice of Battenburg (1914).

165. Worcester Cathedral.

166. The quire of Worcester Cathedral, showing the tomb of John and, beyond, the chantry of Arthur, the elder brother of Henry VIII.

The dissolution of the monastery in 1540 resulted in considerable damage; restoration began in the eighteenth century, but substantive work did not take place until the second half of the following century.

Burial grounds of the rulers of Great Britain.

Chronology of the Rulers
of Great Britain

This list gives the name of the ruler, the dates of the reign and the location of the burial/tomb where known.

EAST ANGLIA

Rædwald	*c.* 599–625	Sutton Hoo
Earpwald	*c.* 616/27–628	
Sigeberht	630–?	
Ecgric		
Anna	?–654	
Æthelhere	654	
Æthelwald	654–664	
Aldwulf	664–713	
Beorna		
Hun		
Alberht		
Æthelred		
Æthelbert		
Æthelstan		
Æthelweard		
Offa	?–*c.* 709	
Edmund (St)	855–870	Bury St Edmund's
Oswald		

ESSEX

Saeberht	*c.* 603–616	Westminster (?)
Sexred	616–617	
Saeweard	617	
Sigeberht I		
Sigeberht II (St)	*c.* 653–664	
Swithelm	*c.* 653–664	
Sighere	664–675	
Sebbi	664–*c.* 694	London
Sigeheard	*c.* 694–*c.* 709	
Swaefred	*c.* 694–*c.* 709	
Saelred	*c.* 709–746	
Swaefberht	?–738	
Sigeric	?–*c.* 798	
Sigered	*c.* 799–*c.* 823	

KENT

Hengist	*c.* 455–*c.* 488
Horsa	?–*c.* 455

Oisc	488–*c.* 512	
Octa		
Eormenric	?–*c.* 560	
Æthelbert I	560–616	Canterbury
Eadbald	616–640	Canterbury
Earconbert	640–664	Canterbury
Ecgbriht I	664–673	Canterbury
Hlothere	673–685	Canterbury
Eadric	685–686	
Suabhard		
Oswini		
Wihtred	690–725	Canterbury
Eadbert	725–748/62	
Æthelbert II	725–762	Reculver
Eardwulf		
Sigered		
Heaberht		
Ecgbriht II	*c.* 765–*c.* 780	
Ealhmund		
Eadbert Praen	796–798	
Cuthred	*c.* 798–807	
Eadwald		
Baldred	?–825	

MERCIA

Penda	*c.* 626/632–654	
Eowa	?–641	
Wulfhere	657–674	Lichfield
Æthelred	674–704	Bardney?
Berhtwald	*c.* 685	
Coenred	704–709	Rome
Ceolred	709–716	Lichfield
Æthelbald	716–757	Repton
Beonred	757	
Offa	757–796	Bedford
Egfrith	787–796	St Albans
Coenwulf	796–821	Winchcombe
Cenelm (St)	821	Winchcombe
Ceolwulf I	821–823	
Beornwulf	823–825	
Ludecan	825–827	
Wiglaf	827–829 & 830–840	Repton
Beorhtwulf	840–852	
Burhed	852–874	Rome
Ceolwulf II	874–?	

NORTHUMBRIA

Æthelfrith	592-616	
Edwin	616–633	Whitby & York
Oswald (St)	634–642	Bardney/Bamborough
Oswine (St)	644–651	Tynemouth
Oswiu	642–670	Whitby
Ecgfrith	670–685	Iona
Aldfrith	685–705	Little Driffield
Ceolwulf (St)	729–737	Norham-on-Tweed
Eadberht	737–758	York
Oswulf	758	

215

Æthelwald	758–765	
Alchred	765–774	
Æthelred I	774–779 & 790–796	
Ælfwald I	779–789	Hexham
Osred II	788–790	Tynemouth
Osbald	796	York
Eardwulf	796–808	
Ælfwald II	808–810	
Eanred	810–841	
Æthelred II	841–844 & 844–849	
Redwulf	844	
Osbert	849–863	
Ælle	863–867	
Egbert I	867–873	
Ricsige	873–876	
Egbert II	876	

WESSEX

Cerdic	519–534	
Cynric	519–560	
Ceawlin	560–591	
Ceol	591–597	
Ceolwulf	597–611	
Cynegils	611–643	Winchester
Cwichelm	626–636	
Cuthred	636–643	
Cenewalh	643–645 & 648–674	Winchester
Seaxburh	642–674	Winchester?
Æscwine	674–676	Winchester
Centwine	676–685	Winchester
Cædwalla	685–688	Rome
Ina	688–726	Rome
Æthelheard	726–741	Winchester
Cuthred	741–754	Winchester
Sigeberht	754–757	Winchester
Cynewulf	757–786	Winchester
Beorhric	786–802	Wareham
Egbert	802–839	Winchester
Æthelwulf	839–855	Winchester
Æthelbald	855–860	Sherborne
Æthelbert	860–866	Sherborne
Æthelred I	866–871	Wimborne
Ælfred	871–899	Winchester
Edward the Elder	899–924	Winchester
Æthelstan	924–939	Malmesbury
Edmund I	939–946	Glastonbury
Eadred	946–955	Winchester
Edwy	955–959	Winchester

ENGLAND

House of Wessex

Edgar	959–975	Glastonbury
Edward the Martyr	975–978	Wareham/Shaftesbury
Æthelred II	978–1013 & 1014–1016	London
Edmund II Ironside	1016	Glastonbury

House of Denmark

Swen	1013–1014	Roskilde
Cnut	1016–1035	Winchester
Harold I Harefoot	1035–1040	Westminster
Harthacnut	1040–1042	Winchester

House of Wessex

Edward the Confessor	1042–1066	Westminster

House of Godwin

Harold II	1066	Waltham Abbey/Bosham?

House of Normandy

William I	1066–1087	Caen
William II	1087–1100	Winchester
Henry I	1100–1135	Reading

House of Blois

Stephen	1135–1154	Faversham

House of Normandy

Mathilda	1141	Rouen

House of Plantagenet

Henry II	1154–1189	Fontevraud
Richard I	1189–1199	Fontevraud
John	1199–1216	Worcester

House of Capet

Louis	1216–1217	St Denis, France

House of Plantagenet

Henry III	1216–1272	Westminster
Edward I	1272–1307	Westminster
Edward II	1307–1327	Gloucester
Edward III	1327–1377	Westminster
Richard II	1377–1399	King's Langley

House of Lancaster

Henry IV	1399–1413	Canterbury
Henry V	1413–1422	Westminster
Henry VI	1422–1461 & 1470–1471	Chertsey

House of York

Edward IV	1461–1470 & 1471–1483	Windsor
Edward V	1483	Westminster?
Richard III	1483–1485	Leicester

House of Tudor

Henry VII	1485–1509	Westminster
Henry VIII	1509–1547	Windsor
Edward VI	1547–1553	Westminster

House of Grey

Jane	1553	London

House of Tudor

Mary I	1553–1558	Westminster
Elizabeth I	1558–1603	Westminster

SCOTLAND

House of MacAlpin

Kenneth I	*c.* 841–*c.* 859	Iona
Donald I	*c.* 859–*c.* 863	Iona
Constantine I	863–877	Iona
Aedh	877–878	Iona
Eochaid	878–889	Iona
Giric I	878–889	Iona
Donald II	889–900	Iona
Constantine II	900–943	St Andrews
Malcolm I	943–954	Iona
Indulf	954–962	Iona
Dubh	962–966/7	Iona
Culen	966/7–971	Iona
Kenneth II	971–995	Iona
Constantine III	995–997	Iona
Kenneth III	997–1005	Iona
Giric II	997–1005	Iona
Malcolm II	1005–1034	Iona

House of Dunkeld

Duncan I	1034–1040	Iona
Macbeth	1040–1057	Iona
Lulach	1057–1058	Iona
Malcolm III	1058–1093	Dunfermline
Donald III	1093–1094 & 1094–1097	Dunkeld/Iona
Duncan II	1094	Iona?
Edmund	1094-1097	
Edgar	1097–1107	Dunfermline
Alexander I	1107–1124	Dunfermline
David I	1124–1153	Dunfermline
Malcolm IV	1153–1165	Dunfermline
William the Lion	1165–1214	Arbroath
Alexander II	1214–1249	Melrose
Alexander III	1249–1286	Dunfermline
Margaret	1286–1290	Bergen, Norway

House of Balliol

John	1292–1296	Bailleul, France

House of Bruce

Robert I	1306–1329	Dunfermline
David II	1329–1371	Holyrood

House of Balliol

Edward	1332–1338	

218

House of Stewart

Robert II	1371–1390	Scone
Robert III	1390–1406	Paisley
James I	1406–1437	Perth
James II	1437–1460	Holyrood
James III	1460–1488	Cambuskenneth
James IV	1488–1513	Sheen
James V	1513–1542	Holyrood
Mary I	1542–1567	Peterborough/Westminster
James VI	1567–1625	see below

ENGLAND AND SCOTLAND/ GREAT BRITAIN

House of Stuart

James VI & I	1603–1625	Westminster
Charles I	1625–1649	Windsor

Commonwealth

Oliver Cromwell	1653–1658	Westminster
Richard Cromwell	1658–1659	Hursley

House of Stuart

Charles II	1660–1685	Westminster
James VII & II	1685–1688	Paris (various)
Mary II	1689–1694	Westminster

House of Orange

William II & III	1689–1702	Westminster

House of Stuart

Anne	1702–1714	Westminster

House of Hanover

George I	1714–1727	Hanover
George II	1727–1760	Westminster
George III	1760–1820	Windsor
George IV	1820–1830	Windsor
William IV	1830–1837	Windsor
Victoria	1837–1901	Windsor

House of Saxe-Coburg-Gotha/ Windsor

Edward VII	1901–1910	Windsor
George V	1910–1936	Windsor
Edward VIII	1936	Windsor
George VI	1936–1952	Windsor
Elizabeth II	1952–	

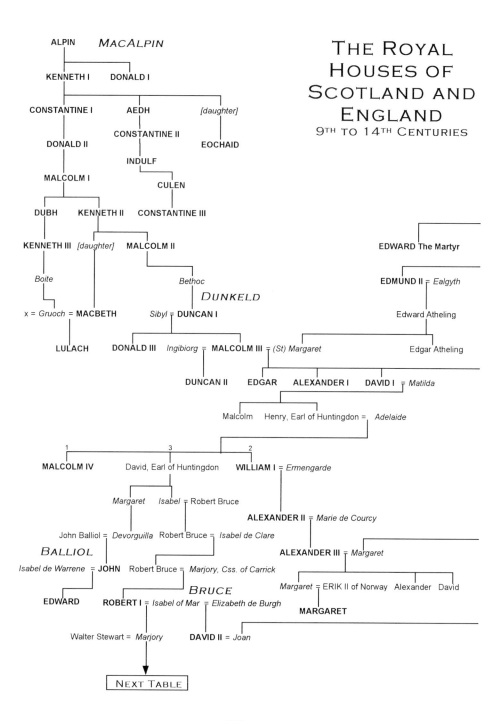

ALPIN   *MacAlpin*

KENNETH I   DONALD I

CONSTANTINE I   AEDH   *[daughter]*

DONALD II   CONSTANTINE II   EOCHAID

INDULF

MALCOLM I   CULEN

DUBH   KENNETH II   CONSTANTINE III

KENNETH III   *[daughter]*   MALCOLM II

Boite   *Bethoc*

Dunkeld

x = *Gruoch* = **MACBETH**   *Sibyl* = **DUNCAN I**

LULACH   DONALD III   *Ingibiorg* = **MALCOLM III** = *(St) Margaret*

DUNCAN II   EDGAR   ALEXANDER I   DAVID I = *Matilda*

Malcolm   Henry, Earl of Huntingdon = *Adelaide*

¹   ³   ²
MALCOLM IV   David, Earl of Huntingdon   **WILLIAM I** = *Ermengarde*

Margaret   *Isabel* = Robert Bruce

John Balliol = *Devorguilla*   Robert Bruce = *Isabel de Clare*   **ALEXANDER II** = *Marie de Courcy*

Balliol   **ALEXANDER III** = *Margaret*

Isabel de Warrene = **JOHN**   Robert Bruce = *Marjory, Css. of Carrick*

Bruce   *Margaret* = ERIK II of Norway   Alexander   David

EDWARD   **ROBERT I** = *Isabel of Mar* = *Elizabeth de Burgh*   **MARGARET**

Walter Stewart = *Marjory*   **DAVID II** = *Joan*

EDWARD The Martyr

EDMUND II = *Ealgyth*

Edward Atheling

Edgar Atheling

THE ROYAL
HOUSES OF
SCOTLAND AND
ENGLAND
9TH TO 14TH CENTURIES

NEXT TABLE

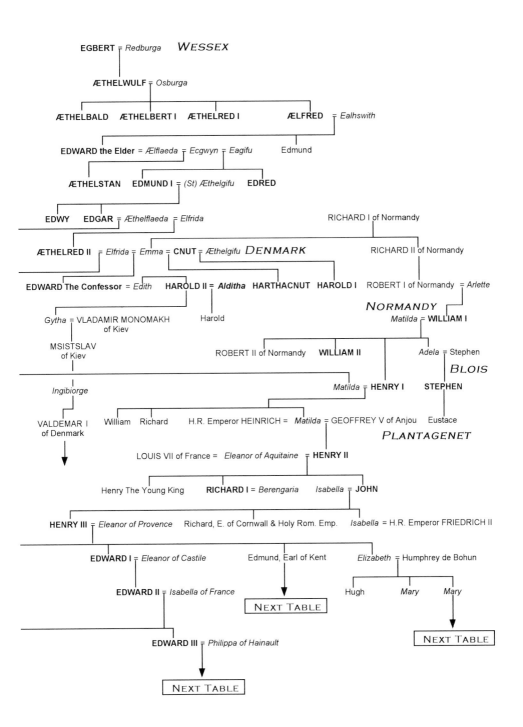

EGBERT = *Redburga*   *WESSEX*

ÆTHELWULF = *Osburga*

ÆTHELBALD   ÆTHELBERT I   ÆTHELRED I   ÆLFRED = *Ealhswith*

EDWARD the Elder = *Ælflaeda* = *Ecgwyn* = *Eagifu*   Edmund

ÆTHELSTAN   EDMUND I = *(St) Æthelgifu*   EDRED

EDWY   EDGAR = *Æthelflaeda* = *Elfrida*   RICHARD I of Normandy

ÆTHELRED II = *Elfrida* = *Emma* = CNUT = *Æthelgifu*   *DENMARK*   RICHARD II of Normandy

EDWARD The Confessor = *Edith*   HAROLD II = *Alditha*   HARTHACNUT   HAROLD I   ROBERT I of Normandy = *Arlette*

NORMANDY

Gytha = VLADAMIR MONOMAKH
of Kiev   Harold   *Matilda* = WILLIAM I

MSISTSLAV
of Kiev   ROBERT II of Normandy   WILLIAM II   *Adela* = Stephen

BLOIS

Ingibiorge   *Matilda* = HENRY I   STEPHEN

VALDEMAR I   William   Richard   H.R. Emperor HEINRICH = *Matilda* = GEOFFREY V of Anjou   Eustace
of Denmark

PLANTAGENET

LOUIS VII of France = *Eleanor of Aquitaine* = HENRY II

Henry The Young King   RICHARD I = *Berengaria*   *Isabella* = JOHN

HENRY III = *Eleanor of Provence*   Richard, E. of Cornwall & Holy Rom. Emp.   *Isabella* = H.R. Emperor FRIEDRICH II

EDWARD I = *Eleanor of Castile*   Edmund, Earl of Kent   *Elizabeth* = Humphrey de Bohun

EDWARD II = *Isabella of France*

NEXT TABLE   Hugh   *Mary*   *Mary*

EDWARD III = *Philippa of Hainault*   NEXT TABLE

NEXT TABLE

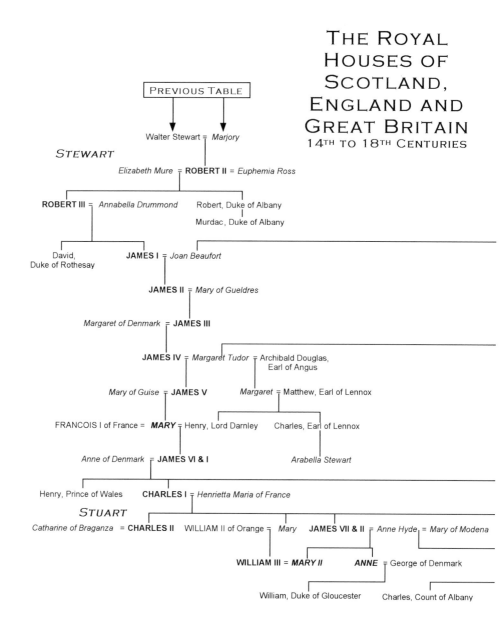

THE ROYAL
HOUSES OF
SCOTLAND,
ENGLAND AND
GREAT BRITAIN
14TH TO 18TH CENTURIES

PREVIOUS TABLE

Walter Stewart ⚭ *Marjory*

STEWART

Elizabeth Mure ⚭ **ROBERT II** = *Euphemia Ross*

ROBERT III ⚭ *Annabella Drummond*   Robert, Duke of Albany

Murdac, Duke of Albany

David,
Duke of Rothesay   **JAMES I** ⚭ *Joan Beaufort*

JAMES II ⚭ *Mary of Gueldres*

Margaret of Denmark ⚭ **JAMES III**

JAMES IV ⚭ *Margaret Tudor* ⚭ Archibald Douglas,
Earl of Angus

Mary of Guise ⚭ **JAMES V**   *Margaret* ⚭ Matthew, Earl of Lennox

FRANCOIS I of France = ***MARY*** ⚭ Henry, Lord Darnley   Charles, Earl of Lennox

Anne of Denmark ⚭ **JAMES VI & I**   *Arabella Stewart*

Henry, Prince of Wales   **CHARLES I** ⚭ *Henrietta Maria of France*

STUART

Catharine of Braganza = **CHARLES II**   WILLIAM II of Orange ⚭ *Mary*   **JAMES VII & II** ⚭ *Anne Hyde* = *Mary of Modena*

WILLIAM III = ***MARY II***   ***ANNE*** ⚭ George of Denmark

William, Duke of Gloucester   Charles, Count of Albany

222

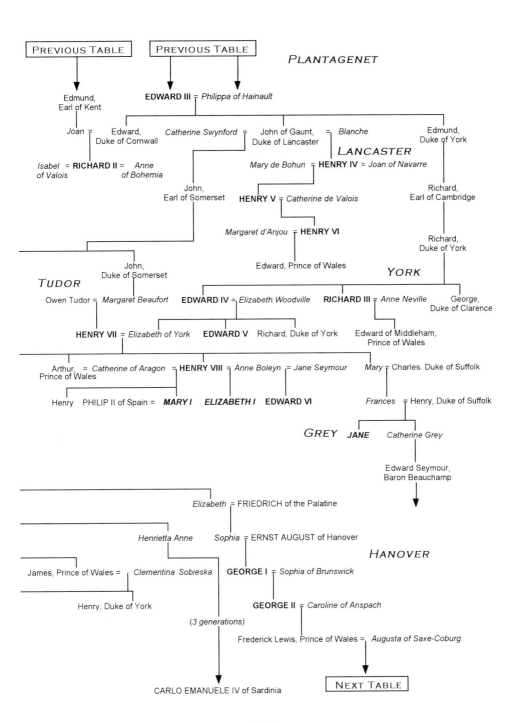

PLANTAGENET

Edmund,
Earl of Kent

EDWARD III = *Philippa of Hainault*

Joan = Edward,   *Catherine Swynford* = John of Gaunt,   = *Blanche*   Edmund,
    Duke of Cornwall   Duke of Lancaster   Duke of York

LANCASTER

Isabel = **RICHARD II** = *Anne*   *Mary de Bohun* = **HENRY IV** = *Joan of Navarre*
of Valois   of Bohemia

John,   **HENRY V** = *Catherine de Valois*   Richard,
Earl of Somerset   Earl of Cambridge

Margaret d'Anjou = **HENRY VI**

Richard,
Duke of York

Edward, Prince of Wales   *YORK*

John,
Duke of Somerset

TUDOR

Owen Tudor = *Margaret Beaufort*   **EDWARD IV** = *Elizabeth Woodville*   **RICHARD III** = *Anne Neville*   George,
                                                                   Duke of Clarence

HENRY VII = *Elizabeth of York*   **EDWARD V**   Richard, Duke of York   Edward of Middleham,
                                                                     Prince of Wales

Arthur, = *Catherine of Aragon* = **HENRY VIII** = *Anne Boleyn* = *Jane Seymour*   *Mary* = Charles. Duke of Suffolk
Prince of Wales

Henry   PHILIP II of Spain =   **MARY I**   **ELIZABETH I**   **EDWARD VI**   *Frances* = Henry, Duke of Suffolk

GREY   **JANE**   *Catherine Grey*

Edward Seymour,
Baron Beauchamp

Elizabeth = FRIEDRICH of the Palatine

Henrietta Anne   *Sophia* = ERNST AUGUST of Hanover   *HANOVER*

James, Prince of Wales =   *Clementina Sobieska*   **GEORGE I** = *Sophia of Brunswick*

Henry, Duke of York   **GEORGE II** = *Caroline of Anspach*

(3 generations)   Frederick Lewis, Prince of Wales = *Augusta of Saxe-Coburg*

CARLO EMANUELE IV of Sardinia   NEXT TABLE

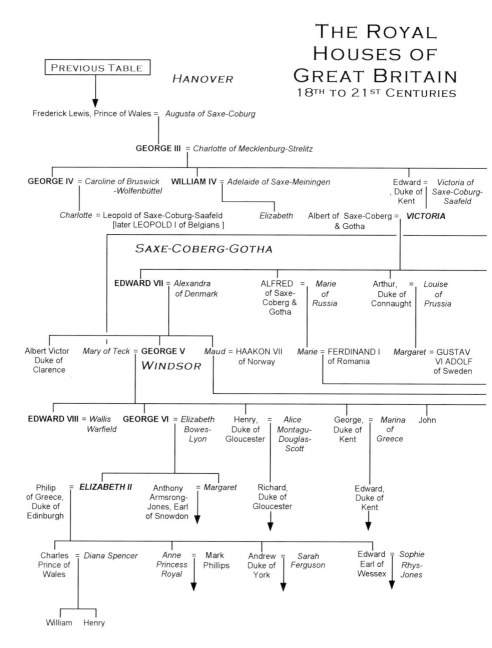

PREVIOUS TABLE

HANOVER

Frederick Lewis, Prince of Wales = *Augusta of Saxe-Coburg*

GEORGE III = *Charlotte of Mecklenburg-Strelitz*

GEORGE IV = *Caroline of Bruswick
-Wolfenbüttel*

WILLIAM IV = *Adelaide of Saxe-Meiningen*

Edward = *Victoria of
, Duke of | Saxe-Coburg-
Kent | Saafeld*

Charlotte = Leopold of Saxe-Coburg-Saafeld
[later LEOPOLD I of Belgians]

Elizabeth

Albert of Saxe-Coberg = **VICTORIA**
& Gotha

SAXE-COBERG-GOTHA

EDWARD VII = *Alexandra
of Denmark*

ALFRED = *Marie
of Saxe-   of
Coberg &   Russia*
Gotha

Arthur, = *Louise
Duke of   of
Connaught   Prussia*

Albert Victor
Duke of
Clarence

Mary of Teck = **GEORGE V**

WINDSOR

Maud = HAAKON VII
of Norway

Marie = FERDINAND I
of Romania

Margaret = GUSTAV
VI ADOLF
of Sweden

EDWARD VIII = *Wallis
Warfield*

GEORGE VI = *Elizabeth
Bowes-
Lyon*

Henry, = *Alice
Duke of   Montagu-
Gloucester Douglas-
Scott*

George, = *Marina
Duke of   of
Kent   Greece*

John

Philip
of Greece,
Duke of
Edinburgh

= **ELIZABETH II**

Anthony
Armsrong-
Jones, Earl
of Snowdon

= *Margaret*

Richard,
Duke of
Gloucester

Edward,
Duke of
Kent

Charles = *Diana Spencer*
Prince of
Wales

*Anne
Princess
Royal*

= Mark
Phillips

Andrew = *Sarah
Duke of   Ferguson*
York

Edward = *Sophie
Earl of   Rhys-
Wessex   Jones*

William   Henry

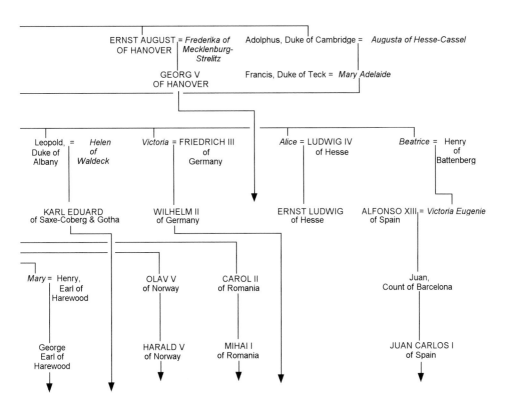

ERNST AUGUST = *Frederika of*   Adolphus, Duke of Cambridge = *Augusta of Hesse-Cassel*
OF HANOVER   *Mecklenburg-*
             Strelitz

GEORG V   Francis, Duke of Teck = *Mary Adelaide*
OF HANOVER

Leopold, = *Helen*   *Victoria* = FRIEDRICH III   *Alice* = LUDWIG IV   *Beatrice* = Henry
Duke of   *of*   of   of Hesse   of
Albany   *Waldeck*   Germany   Battenberg

KARL EDUARD   WILHELM II   ERNST LUDWIG   ALFONSO XIII = *Victoria Eugenie*
of Saxe-Coberg & Gotha   of Germany   of Hesse   of Spain

Mary = Henry,   OLAV V   CAROL II   Juan,
         Earl of   of Norway   of Romania   Count of Barcelona
         Harewood

George   HARALD V   MIHAI I   JUAN CARLOS I
Earl of   of Norway   of Romania   of Spain
Harewood

Bibliography

Abbreviations

Arch = *Archaeologia: Or Miscellaneous Tracts Relating to Antiquity* (London).
ARSFStG = *Annual Report of the Society of Friends of St George's and the Descendants of the Knights of the Garter* (Windsor).
JBAA = *Journal of the British Archaeological Association* (London).
PSAS = *Proceedings of the Society of Antiquaries of Scotland* (Edinburgh).
RCHM = Royal Commission on Historical Monuments (England).
ScotAnt = *The Scottish Antiquary; or, Northern Notes and Queries* (Edinburgh).
TSAS = *Transactions of the Society of Antiquaries of Scotland* (Edinburgh).

Studies of individual royal burials

Rulers are listed in alphabetical order. Mentions in works dealing with a wide range of burials (Begent 1992 [Windsor]; Duffy 2003 [English kings from 1066 to 1509]; Marsden 1994 [Iona]; Oxley 1996 [Windsor]; Royal Commission on Historical Monuments (England) 1924; Stanley 1882 [both Westminster]; Wall 1891 [English kings in general]) are not separately detailed below.

Ælfred: Howard 1800; Quirk 1961.
Æscwine: Willis 1845: 5.
Æthelbald of Mercia: Taylor 1989.
Æthelred I of Wessex: Coulstock 1993.
Æthelred II: Sinclair 1909: 93.
Æthelwulf: Crook (ed.) 1993; Crook 1999; Rumble (ed.) 1994: 166-92.
Aldfrith: Langdale 1822; Baines 1823.
Alexander I: Chalmers 1844.
Cenewalh: Willis 1845: 5.
Centwine: Willis 1845: 5.
Charles I: Fellowes 1950; Halford 1813; Partridge 1998.
Charles 'III': Anon 1939; http://www.jacobite.ca/kings/charles3.htm
Cnut: Biddle and Kjolbye-Biddle 2003; Crook (ed.) 1993: 275-8; Crook 1994; 1999; Rumble (ed.) 1994: 166-92.
Cynegils: Crook (ed.) 1993; Crook 1999; Rumble (ed.) 1994: 166-92; Willis 1845: 5.
Cynewulf: Crook (ed.) 1993; Crook 1999; Rumble (ed.) 1994: 166-92.
David I: Chalmers 1844.
Edgar of Scots: Chalmers 1844.
Edmund (St) of East Anglia: Houghton 1970; Scarfe 1970; 1986: 55-71.
Edmund II 'Ironside': Crook (ed.) 1993: 298 n. 44.
Eadred: Crook (ed.) 1993; Crook 1999; Rumble (ed.) 1994: 166-92; Wall 1891: 163-5.
Edward the Confessor: O'Neilly and Tanner 1966; Taylour 1685; Tanner 1954; Westlake 1916.

Edward the Elder: Quirk 1961.

Edward the Martyr: Chandler 2003; Cubitt 2000; Harden 1954; Keen 1999; Kite 1862: 274; Rollason 1983; Stowell 1970.

Edward I: Ayloffe 1775; Bradford 1933: 102-3; Steane 1993: 55.

Edward II: Bradford 1933: 106; Cuttino and Lyman 1978; Westmacott 1860.

Edward III: Plenderleith and Maryon 1959.

Edward IV: Anon. 1770; Blackburne and Bond 1962: 29-30; Carliol, Emlyn and Lind 1790; Lysons and Lysons 1813: 724*-5*; Roberts 1976–77; Tanner and Wright 1935.

Edward V: Steane 1993: 65-6; Tanner and Wright 1935; White 1959; Hammond and White 2000.

Edward VII: Bond 1958: 67.

Egbert: Crook (ed.) 1993; Crook 1999; Rumble (ed.) 1994: 166-92.

Elizabeth I: Bradford 1933: 170.

George II: Cocke 2001; Tanner 1969: 178-9.

George V: Bond 1958.

George VI: Pace, G.G. 1968-9; Pace, P. 1990: 217-22.

Harold II: Marwood 1954; Pollock 1996.

Harthacnut: Crook (ed.) 1993: 264-6; Crook 1999; Rumble (ed.) 1994.

Henry I: Nares 1817; Giding 1890.

Henry II: Anon 1867; Boase 1971; Hallet 1902; James 1991.

Henry III: Bradford 1933: 63-4; 80-1; Hanna 1916–17; Plenderleith and Maryon 1959; Stanley 1880.

Henry IV: Spry 1836.

Henry V: St John Hope 1913–14; Steane 1993.

Henry VI: Begent 1992: 33-4; Hope 1911; White 1982.

Henry VII: Higgins 1894; Plenderleith and Maryon 1959; Tatton-Brown and Mortimer, 2003.

Henry VIII: Anon. 1965; Bradford 1933: 139; Colvin, Ransome and Summerson 1975: 219-22, 320-2; Halford 1813; Higgins 1894; Nash 1789; Partridge 1998.

Henry 'I & IX': Anon 1939; http://www.jacobite.ca/kings/henry.htm

James I of Scots: Bradford 1933: 44; Fawcett n.d.; Fittis 1885: 220-48; R[oss] 1897.

James III: Alexander 1868.

James IV: Cloake 1977; Norman 1902; Stow 1598: 112.

James V: Pearson 1928: 36-47.

James 'VIII & III': Anon 1939; http://www.jacobite.ca/kings/james3.htm

Jane: Bell 1877: 52-3; 176.

John of England: Green 1797; Pafford 1958.

Malcolm I: Stuart 1818.

Malcolm III: Henderson 1856; Stuart 1859.

Malcolm IV: Chalmers 1844.

Mary I of England: Bradford 1933: 150-1.

Oliver Cromwell: Pearson and Morant 1934; Stanley 1869: 630.

Oswald (St) of Mercia: Fowler 1900; Heighway and Bryant 1999.

Rædwald: Carver 1998.

Richard I: Boase 1971; Bradford 1933: 65-6; Fagnen 1992; Hallet 1902; Way 1842.

Richard II: Ayloffe 1775; Conway of Allington 1932; King 1782: 315; Nichols 1841; Plenderleith and Maryon 1959; Stanley 1880.

Richard III: Baldwin 1986.

Richard Cromwell: Rawdon 1993.

Robert I: Chalmers 1844: 126-50; Henderson 1856; Jardine 1822; Johnston 1878; Pearson 1924; Williams 2004.

Robert III: Boog 1818.

Saeberht: Lakin 2004.
Stephen: Philip 1969.
Victoria: Ward-Jackson 1993.
Wiglaf: Taylor 1989.
William II: Crook 1999; Joyce 1869; [Richards] 1870; Willis 1845: 18-19.

General bibliography

Anon. 1965. 'The Opening of the Tomb of King Charles I in 1888', *ARSFStG* IV/6: 229-30.
Anon. 1939. 'Resting-Place of the Last Stuarts: New Tomb in St. Peter's', *The Times* (21 March 1939): 19d.
Adams, M. and Reeve, J. 1987. 'Excavations at Spitalfields', *Antiquity* 61: 252-3.
[Anstis, T.] 1770. 'An Extract relating to the Burial of K. Edward IV. From a MS. of the late Mr. Anstis, now in the Possession of Thomas Astle, Esquire', *Arch* I: 348-9.
Alexander, Sir J.E. 1868. 'An Account of the Excavations at Cambuskenneth Abbey in May 1864', *PSAS* 6: 20-2.
Allington, Lord Conway of 1932. 'Episodes in a Varied Life', *Country Life* LXXI/1846 (4 June 1932): 622.
Ariès, P. 1976. *Western Attitudes towards Death from the Middle Ages to the Present* (London).
Ariès, P. 1981. *The Hour of our Death* (London): 165-70.
Ayloffe, Sir J. 1775. 'An Account of the Body of King Edward the First, as it appeared on the opening of his Tomb in the Year 1774', *Arch* III: 376-413.
Baines, E. 1823. *History, Directory & Gazetteer, of the County of York* (Leeds).
Baldwin, D. 1986. 'King Richard's Grave at Leicester', *Leicestershire Archaeological and Historical Society Transactions* LX: 21-4.
Beard, C.R. 1933. *The Romance of Treasure Trove* (London): 188-93.
Begent, P.J. 1992. *The Romance of St George's Chapel, Windsor Castle*, 15th ed. (Windsor).
Bell, D.C. 1877. *Notices of the Historic Persons Buried in the Chapel of St Peter ad Vincula in the Tower of London* (London).
Biddle, M. 1970. *The Old Minster. Excavations Near Winchester Cathedral, 1961–1969* (Winchester).
Biddle, M. 1976. *Winchester in the Early Middle Ages* (Oxford).
Biddle, M. and Kjolbye-Biddle, B. 2003. 'Knud den Store og hans familie', in K. Kryger (ed.) *Selskabet til Udgivilse af Danske Mindesmaerke* (Copenhagen).
Blackburne, H.W. and Bond, M.F. 1962. *The Romance of St George's Chapel, Windsor Castle*, 6th ed. (Windsor).
Bland, Olivia 1986. *The Royal Way of Death* (London).
Boase, T.S.R. 1971. 'Fontévrault and the Plantagenets', *JBAA* 3rd ser. XXIV: 1-10.
Bond, S.M. 1958. *The Monuments of St George's Chapel* (Windsor).
Boog, Rev. Dr 1818. 'Account of Queen Bleary's Tomb in the Abbey Church of Paisley', *TSAS* 2: 456-61.
Bradford, C.A. 1933. *Heart Burial* (London).
Brewer, C. 2000. *The Death of Kings: A Medical History of the Kings and Queens of England* (London).
Brooke-Hunt, V. 1904. *The Story of Westminster Abbey* (London).
Brown, E.A.R. 1981. 'Death and the Human Body in the Later Middle Ages: The Legislation of Boniface VIII on the Division of the Corpse', *Viator, Medieval and Renaissance Studies* 12 (Los Angeles): 221-70.
Bruce-Mitford, R. 1975–83. *The Sutton Hoo Ship Burial*, 3 vols (London).
Carliol, J., Emlyn, H. and Lind, J. 1790. 'The Vault, Body, and Monument, of EDWARD IV in St George's Chapel at Windsor', *Vetusta Monumenta* III: pl. VII-VIII.

Bibliography

Carment Lanfry, A.M. 1977. *La Cathédrale Notre-Dame de Rouen* (Rouen).

Carver, M. 1998. *Sutton Hoo: Burial Ground of Kings?* (London).

Chalmers P. 1844, 1859. *Historical and Statistical Account of Dunfermline*, 2 vols (Edinburgh).

Chandler. J. 2003. *A Higher Reality: The History of Shaftesbury's Royal Nunnery* (East Knoyle).

Cloake, J. 1977. 'The Charterhouse of Sheen', *Surrey Archaeological Collections* 71: 145-98.

Cocke, T. 2001. ' "The Repository of our English Kings": The Henry VII Chapel as Royal Mausoleum', *Architectural History* 44: 212-20.

Colvin, H.M., Ransome, D.R. and Summerson, J. 1975. *The History of the King's Works*, III. *1485–1660*, part 1 (London): 219-22, 320-2.

Cook, O. 1997 'Head Case', *Cambridge Alumni Magazine*, Easter 1997: 40.

Coulstock, P.H. 1993. *The Collegiate Church of Wimborne Minster* (Woodbridge).

Crook, J. 1994. 'The bones of King Cnut', in A. Rumble (ed.), *The Reign of Cnut: King of England, Denmark and Norway* (London): 165-92.

Crook, J. 1999. 'The Rufus tomb in Winchester Cathedral', *Antiquaries Journal* 79: 187-212.

Crook, J. (ed.) 1993. *Winchester Cathedral: 900 Years* (Chichester).

Crull, J. 1711 & 1713. *Antiquities of Westminster Abbey* (London).

Cubitt, C. 2000. 'Sites and Sanctity: Revisiting the Cult of Murdered and Martyred Anglo-Saxon Royal Saints', *Early Medieval Europe* 9: 53-83.

Cuttino, G.P. and Lyman, T.W. 1978. 'Where is Edward II?', *Speculum* 53: 522-43.

Darr, A.P. 1979. 'The Sculptures of Torrigiano', *The Connoisseur* 20: 177f.

Dart, J. 1723. *Westmonasterium or The History & Antiquities of the Abbey Church of St Peters Westminster*, 2 vols (London).

Dodson, A.M. 1994. 'The King is Dead', in C. Eyre, A. Leahy and L.M. Leahy (eds), *The Unbroken Reed: Studies in the Culture and Heritage of Ancient Egypt In Honour of A.F. Shore* (London): 71-95.

Dorment, R. 1986. *Alfred Gilbert: Sculptor and Goldsmith* (London).

Duffy, M. 2003. *Royal Tombs of Medieval England* (Stroud).

Ellis, R.S. 1860. 'An Account of the Later Years of James Hepburn, Earl of Bothwell: his Imprisonment and Death in Denmark and the Disinterment of his Presumed Remains', *Arch* 38: 308-21.

Erlande-Brandenburg, A. 1968. 'Le tombeau de Saint Louis', *Bulletin Monumental* CXXVI, I: 7-36.

Fagnen, C. 1992. *Fontevraud: Histoire-Archéologie* 1 (Fontevraud): 23-32.

Fawcett, R. n.d. *Guide to St John's Kirk* (Perth).

Fellowes, E.H. 1950. *Memoranda Concerning King Charles I* (Windsor).

Fenwick, H. 1978. *Scotland's Abbeys and Cathedrals* (London).

Fittis, R.S. 1885. *Ecclesiastical Annals of Perth, to the Period of the Reformation* (Edinburgh).

Fletcher, J.M.J. 1919. 'The Tomb of King Ethelred in Wimborne Minster', *Proceedings of the Dorset Natural History and Archaeological Society* 40: 24-34.

Fowler, J.T. 1900. 'On an Examination of the Grave of St Cuthbert in Durtham Cathedral Church, in March 1899', *Arch* 57: 11-28.

Fuller, T. 1868. *The Church History of Britain from the Birth of Jesus Christ until the Year MCCXLVIII*[3] (London): III, 567-7.

Gardner, A. 1940. *Alabaster Tombs of the Pre-Reformation Period in England* (Cambridge).

Gidding, J.M. 1890. 'Henry the First's Tomb in Reading Abbey', *Journal of the Berkshire Archaeological Society* 4: 95-9.

Gough, R. 1786; 1796ff. *Sepulchral Monuments in Great Britain … from the Norman Conquest to the Seventeenth Century*, 2 vols (London).

Green, V. 1796, *History and Antiquities of the City and Suburbs of Worcester*, 2 vols (Worcester).

Green, V. 1797. *An Account of the Discovery of the Body of King John in the Cathedral Church of Worcester, July 17th 1797* (London/Worcester).

Greenwood, D. 1982/1990. *Who's Buried Where in England* (London).

Guibert, P. 1639. *The Charitable Physitian …* (London).

Halford, Sir H. 1813. *An Account of What Appeared on Opening the Coffin of King Charles the First in the Vault of King Henry the Eighth in St George's Chapel at Windsor on the First of April M DCCC XIII* (London).

Hallam, E.M. 1991. 'The Eleanor Crosses and Royal Burial Customs', *Eleanor of Castille 1290–1990* (Stamford): 9-22.

Hallet, C. 1902. 'The Last Resting Place of our Angevin Kings', *The Nineteenth Century*, August 1902: 265-81.

Hammond, P.W. and White, W.J. 2000. 'The Sons of Edward IV: A Re-examination of the Evidence on their Deaths and on the Bones in Westminster Abbey', in P.W. Hammond (ed.), *Richard III, Loyalty, Lordship and Law* (London).

Hanna, J.M. 1916–17. 'Notes on the Royal Heart Preserved at St Margaret's Convent, Whitehouse Loan, Edinburgh', *PSAS* 5th ser. 3: 16-23.

Harden, D.B. 1954. 'A Glass Bowl of Dark Age Date and Some Medieval Grave-Finds from Shaftesbury Abbey', *Antiquaries' Journal* XXXIV: 188-94.

Hastings, J.M. 1946. 'The Tomb of Edward II at Gloucester', *Architectural Review* 49: 121ff.

Heighway C. and Bryant, R. *The Golden Minster. The Anglo-Saxon Minster and Later Medieval Priory of St Oswald at Gloucester* (York).

Henderson, E. 1856. *The Royal Tombs at Dunfermline* (Dunfermline).

Higgins, A. 1894. 'On the work of Florentine Sculptors in England in the Early Part of the Sixteenth Century: With Special Reference to the Tombs of Cardinal Wolsey and King Henry VIII', *Archaeological Journal* LI: 152-90.

Houghton, B.R.S. 1970. *St Edmund, King and Martyr* (Lavenham).

Howard, H. 1800. 'Enquiries Concerning the Tomb of King Alfred, at Hyde Abbey, near Winchester', *Arch* 13: 309-12.

Howgrave-Graham, R.P. 1961. 'The Earlier Royal Funeral Effigies: New Light on Portraiture in Westminster Abbey', *Arch* 98: 159-82.

Hyde, H. and Gale, S. 1723. *The History and Antiquities of the Cathedral Church of Winchester* (London).

Jacob, E.F. 1961. *The Fifteenth Century* (Oxford).

James, F.-C. 1991. 'The Abbey and the Plantagenets: A Family Business', in Martin-Bagnaudez (ed.) 1991: 17-21.

Jardine, H. 1822. 'Extracts from the Report Relative to the Tomb of King Robert Bruce, and the Church of Dunfermline', *Archaeologia Scotia* II: 435ff.

Johnston, T.B. 1878. 'The Story of the Fabrication of the "Coffin-Plate" Said to have been Found in the Tomb of King Robert Bruce in Dunfermline Abbey', *PSAS* 12: 466-71.

Joyce J.G. 1869. 'On the Opening and Removal of a Tomb in Winchester Cathedral, Reputed to be that of King William Rufus', *Arch* 42: 309-21.

Keen, L. (ed.) 1999. *Studies in the Early History of Shaftesbury Abbey* (Dorchester).

Keen, L. and Scarff, E. (eds) 2002. *Windsor, Medieval Archaeology, Art & Architecture in the Thames Valley* (Leeds).

K[eepe], H. 1683. *Monumenta Westmonasteriensa, or a Historic Account of the Original Increase, and Present State of St Peter's or, The Abbey Church of Westminster* (London).

Kempe, A.J. 1836. 'Some Account of the Jerusalem Chamber in the Abbey of Westminster, and of the Painted Glass Remaining Therein', *Arch* 26: 432-40.

King, E. 1782. 'Sequel to the Observations on Ancient Castles', *Arch* VI: 231-375.

Kite, E. 1862. 'Recent Excavations on the Site of Shaftesbury Abbey', *Wiltshire Archaeological and Natural History Magazine* VII: 272-7.

Laing, D. 1855. 'Notices of the Funeral of James, Second Earl of Murray', *PSAS* I: 191-6.

Laing, D. 1866. 'Notes Relating to the Interment of James III of Scotland and of his Queen, Margaret of Denmark, in the Abbey Church of Cambuskenneth', *PSAS* 6: 26-33.

Lakin, D. 2004. 'The Prittlewell Royal Anglo-Saxon Burial', *Minerva* 15/3.

Litton, J. 1991. *The English Way of Death* (London).

Langdale, T. 1822. *A Topographical Dictionary of Yorkshire*, 2nd ed. (Northallerton).

Lysons, D and Lyson, S. 1813. *Magna Britannia, A Concise Topographical Account of the Several Counties of Great Britain* (London).

Marsden, J. 1994. *The Tombs of the Kings: An Iona Book of the Dead* (Felinfach).

Martin-Bagnaudez, J. (ed.) 1991. *Fontevarud* (*Notre Histoire* Special 22).

Marwood, G. 1954. *The Stone Coffins of Bosham Church* (privately printed).

Moore, S.A. 1888. 'Documents Relating to the Death and Burial of Edward II', *Arch* L: 215-26.

Nares, R. 1817. 'Observations on the Discovery of Part of a Sarcophagus at Reading Abbey, in Berkshire, supposed to have contained the Remains of King Henry I', *Arch* XVIII: 272-4.

Nash, T. 1789. 'Observations on the Time of the Death and Place of Burial of Queen Katharine Parr', *Arch* 9: 1-9.

Neale, J.P. and Brayley, E.W. 1818. *The History and Antiquities of the Abbey Church of St Peter Westminster*, 2 vols (London).

Nichols, J.G. 1841. 'Observations on the Heraldic Devices Discovered on the Effigies of Richard the Second and his Queen in Westminster Abbey', *Arch* XXIX: 32-59.

Norman, P. 1902. 'On the Destroyed Church of St Michael Wood Street, in the City of London, with some Notes on the Church of St Michael Massishaw', *Arch* 58: 189-216.

O'Neilly, J.G. and Tanner, L.E. 1966. 'The Shrine of St Edward the Confessor', *Arch* 100: 129-54.

Oxley, N.E. 1996. *A.Y. Nutt: In Service to Three Monarchs at Windsor* (Windsor).

Pace, P. 1990. *The Architecture of George Pace* (London).

Pace, G.G. 1968-9. 'King George VI Memorial Chapel, St George's Chapel, Windsor Castle', *ARSFStG* IV/10: 421-5.

Pafford, J.H.F. 1958. 'King John's Tomb in Worcester Cathedral: An Account of its Opening in 1529 by John Bale', *Transactions of the Worcestershire Archaeological Society* ns XXXV: 58-60.

Partridge, R.B. 1998. *'O Horrable Murder': The Trial, Execution and Burial of King Charles I* (London).

Pearson, K. 1924. 'The Skull of Robert the Bruce, King of Scotland 1274–1329', *Biometrika* 16: 253-72.

Pearson, K. 1928. 'The Skull and Portraits of Henry Stewart, Lord Darnley', *Biometrika* 20B: 1-104.

Pearson, K. and Morant, G.M. 1934. 'The Wilkinson Head of Oliver Cromwell and its Relationship to Busts, Masks and Painted Portraits', *Biometrika* 26: 269-378.

Peers, C. and Tanner, L.E. 1949. 'On Some Recent Discoveries in Westminser Abbey, I: The Bohun Tomb in St. John the Baptist's Chapel', *Arch* 93: 151-5.

Philip, B. 1969. *Excavations at Faversham, 1965. The Royal Abbey, Roman Villa and Belgic Farmstead* (Kent Archaeological Research Council).

Plenderleith, H.J. and H. Maryon 1959. 'The Royal Bronze Effigies in Westminster Abbey', *Antiquaries Journal* 39: 87-90.

Pollock, J. 1996. *A Speculative Guide to Bosham Church c. 1066* (Bosham).

Quirk, R.N. 1961. 'Winchester New Minster and its Tower', *JBAA* 3rd ser. 24: 16-54.

Rahtz, P. 1993. *The English Heritage Book of Glastonbury* (London).

Ramm, H.G., Black, D.W., Wormold, F., Oman, C., Werner, A.E.A. and Summers, G.A.C. 1971. 'The Tombs of the Archbishops Walter de Gray (1216–55) and Godfrey de Ludian (1258–65) in York Minster, and their Contents', *Arch* 103: 101-48.

Sawdon, S.C. 1993. *All Saints' Church Hursley: A History & Guide* (Ampfield).

[Richards, F.W.] 1870. *William Rufus: His Tomb* (London).

Roberts, J. 1976–77. 'Henry Emlyn's Restoration of St George's Chapel', *ARSFStG* V/8: 331-8.

Rollason, D.W. 1983. 'The Cults of Murdered Royal Saints in Anglo-Saxon England', *Anglo-Saxon England* 11: 1-22.

R[oss], T. 1897. 'The Tombstones of King James I. of Scotland and his Queen', *ScotAnt* XI: 64.

Royal Commission on Historical Monuments (England) 1921. *An Inventory of Historical Monuments in Essex*, II (London: HMSO).

Royal Commission on Historical Monuments (England) 1924. *An Inventory of Historical Monuments in London*, I: *Westminster Abbey* (London: HMSO).

Royal Commission on Historical Monuments (England) 1952. *An Inventory of the Historical Monuments in the County of Dorset*, I (London: HMSO).

Royal Commission on Historical Monuments (England) 1972, *An Inventory of Historical Monuments in the County of Dorset*, IV: *North Dorset* (London: HMSO).

Royal Commission on Historical Monuments (England) 1972. *An Inventory of Historical Monuments in London*, IV: *City of London* (London: HMSO).

Royal Commission on Historical Monuments (England) 1975, *An Inventory of Historical Monuments in the County of Dorset*, V: *East Dorset* (London: HMSO).

Sagastibelza, M. 2003. 'La tumba de Berenguela', http://www.ctv.es/sagastibelza/berenguela/berenguela_tumba.htm.

Scarfe, N. 1970. 'The Body of St Edmund: An Essay in Necrobiography', *Proceedings of the Suffolk Institute of Archaeology and History* 31: 303-17.

Scarfe, N. 1986. *Suffolk in the Middle Ages: Studies in Places and Place-names, the Sutton Hoo Ship Burial, Saints, Mummies and Crosses, Domesday Book, and Chronicles of Bury Abbey* (Woodbridge).

Sinclair, W.M. 1909. *Memorials of St Paul's Cathedral* (London).

Spry, J.H. 1836. 'A Brief Account of the Examination of the Tomb of King Henry IV in the Cathedral of Canterbury, August 21, 1832', *Arch* 26: 440-5.

St John Hope, W.H. 1907. 'On the Funeral Effigies of the Kings and Queens of England, with Special Reference to Those in the Abbey Church of Westminster', *Arch* 60: 517-65.

St John Hope, W.H. 1911. 'The Discovery of the Remains of King Henry VI in St George's Chapel, Windsor Castle', *Arch* 62: 533-42.

St John Hope, W.H. 1913. 'Windsor Castle', *Country Life*: 482-4.

St John Hope, W.H. 1913–14. 'The Funeral, Monument and Chantry Chapel of King Henry the Fifth', *Arch* 45: 129-86.

Stanley, A.P. 1869. *Historical Memorials of Westminster Abbey*, 3rd ed. (London).

Stanley, A.P. 1880. 'On an Examination of the Tombs of Richard II and Henry III in Westminster Abbey', *Arch* 45: 309-27.

Stanley, A.P. 1881. 'On the Depositions of the Remains of Katharine de Valois, Queen of Henry V in Westminster Abbey', *Arch* 46: 281-96.

Stanley, A.P. 1882. *Historical Memorials of Westminster Abbey*, 5th ed. (London).

Steane, J. 1993. *The Archaeology of the Medieval English Monarchy* (London: Batsford).

Stone, L. 1955/1972. *Sculpture in Britain. The Middle Ages* (Harmondsworth: Penguin).

Stothard, C.A. 1817. *The Monumental Effigies of Great Britain* (London).

Stow, J. 1592. *The Annales of England ... From the First Inhabitation until this Present Yeere 1592* (London).

Stow, J. 1598. *A Survey of London, Written in the Year 1598* (reprinted Oxford, 1971).

Stowell, T.E.A. 1970. 'The Bones of Edward the Martyr', *The Criminologist* 5: 141-60.

Stuart, Professor 1818. 'Account of the Discovery of an Ancient Tomb at Fetteresso in Kincardineshire in January 1822', *TSAS* 2: 462-5.

Stuart, J. 1859. 'Notices of the Burial of King Malcolm III in the Monastery at Tynmouth in 1093, and of the Subsequent History of the Remains', *PSAS* II: 81-9.

Tanner, J.D. 1953. 'Tombs of Royal Babes in Westminster Abbey', *JBAA* 3rd Ser. 16: 25-40.

Tanner, L.E. 1954. 'The Quest for the Cross of St Edward the Confessor', *JBAA* 3rd Ser. 17: 1-11.

Tanner, L.E. and Clapham, A.W. 1933. 'Recent Discoveries in the Nave of Westminster Abbey', *Arch* 83: 227ff.

Tanner, L.E. and Wright, W. 1935. 'Recent Investigations Regarding the Fate of the Princes in the Tower', *Arch* 84: 1-26.

Tatton-Brown, T. and Mortimer, R. 2003. *Westminster Abbey: The Lady Chapel of Henry VII* (Woodbridge).

Taylor, H.M. 1989. *St Wystan's Church Repton* (Repton).

Taylour, C. [H. Keepe] 1685. *A True and Perfect Narrative of the Strange and Unexpected Finding of the Crucifix & Gold-Chain of That Pious Prince, St Edward the King and Confessor, Which was found after 620 Years Interment: And Presented to His Most Sacred Majesty King James the Second* (London).

Wall, J.C. 1891. *The Tombs of the Kings of England* (London).

Ward-Jackson, P. 1993. 'The French Background of Royal Monuments at Windsor and Frogmore', *Church Monuments* VIII: 63-83.

Way, A. 1842. 'Effigy of King Richard, Coeur de Lion, in the Cathedral of Rouen', *Arch* 29: 202-16.

Wendebourg, E.-A. 1986. *Westminster Abbey als königliche Grablage zwischen 1250 und 1400* (Worms).

Westlake, H.F. 1916a. '[O]n a Recent Examination of the Shrine of St Edward at Westminster', *Proc. Soc. Ant.* 2nd ser. XXVIII: 68-77.

Westmacott, R. 1860. 'On the Monument of King Edward II and Mediaeval Sculpture', *Arch. Journal* 17: 297-310.

White, G.H. 1959. 'The Princes in the Tower', *Complete Peerage* XII, part II, Appendix J: 32-9.

White, W.J. 1982. 'The Death and Burial of Henry VI. A Review of the Facts and Theories, Part I', *Ricardian* VI/78 Sept.: 70-7.

Williams, D. 2004. 'From Constantine the Great to Robert the Bruce: the Elgin Porphyry', *Minerva* 15/1: 40-2.

Williamson, A. 1981. *The Mystery of the Princes* (London.

Willis, R. 1845 *The Architectural History of Winchester Cathedral* (reprinted 1984, Winchester).

Wilson, D. 1863. 'Notes on the Search for the Tomb of the Royal Foundress of the Collegiate Church of the Holy Trinity at Edinburgh', *PSAS* IV: 554-65.

Wilson-Claridge, J. n.d. *Report of Excavation on the Site of the Royal Abbey Church of Our Lady and St Eadward the Martyr at Shaftesbury AD 1930-1* (Gloucester and London).

Worsaae, J.J.A. 1862. 'Bothwell's Grav i Farreveile Kirke', *Illustreret Tidende* 123: 145-8.

Sources of Illustrations

Brooke-Hunt 1904: 5, 52, 117.
Carliol, Emlyn and Lind 1790 (adapted from): 7.
Dart 1723: 6; 77.
Dean and Chapter of Westminster: 1, 39, 40, 42, 46, 47, 48, 49, 51, 60, 61, 62, 68, 70, 98, 99, 146, 149, 150, 151.
Aidan Dodson: 2, 8, 10, 11, 12, 17, 18, 20, 22, 23, 28, 30, 32, 33, 34, 41, 45, 58, 59, 69, 74, 75, 76, 78, 79, 80, 81, 82, 83, 84, 85, 86, 87, 88, 89, 90, 91, 92, 93, 94, 95, 96, 97, 100, 101, 102, 107, 112, 113, 115, 116, 118, 121, 122, 123, 124, 125, 127, 128, 129, 131, 132, 133, 134, 135, 136, 138, 139, 140, 141, 142, 143, 144, 145, 147, 148, 149, 151, 152, 153, 156, 157, 160, 161, 162, 163, 164, 165, 167.
Aidan Dodson, after Philip 1969: 31.
Aidan Dodson, courtesy Dean & Canons of Windsor: 53, 54, 55, 56, 57, 103, 104, 108, 109, 110, 111, 114, 158, 159.
Aidan Dodson, courtesy Dean & Chapter of Canterbury: 50, 126.
Aidan Dodson, courtesy Dean & Chapter of Winchester: 4, 14, 16, 21, 25, 26, 29, 154, 155.
Aidan Dodson, courtesy Dean & Chapter of Worcester: 37, 166.
Fowler 1900: 13.
Green 1797: 38.
Higgins 1894 (after): 64.
Illustrated London News Picture Library: 106.
Museum of London: 73
A.Y. Nutt, courtesy Dean & Canons of Windsor: 65, 105.
J. O'Neilly, courtesy Dean and Chapter of Westminster: 27.
Pearson 1928: 19.
Pearson and Morant 1934: 3.
Shaftesbury Abbey & Museum Trust Archives: 24.
Society of Antiquaries, London: 43, 44.
Stanley 1882: 63, 66, 67, 71, 72.
Trustees of the British Museum: 9.
Wall 1891: 15.
Way 1842: 35, 36.
Winchester Museums Service: 19.
Worsaae 1862: 120.

Index

Rulers of British kingdoms appear in **bold**; appearances in the chronology on pp. 214-19, and in the genealogies on pp. 220-5, are not included in this index.

Abel-Smith, Sir Henry (d. 1983: great-grandson-in-law of Victoria) 210-11

Abercorn, Duchess of: see Hamilton

Addison, Joseph (1672–1719) 192-3

Adela of Louvain, Queen (wife of Henry I) 151

Adelaide of Saxe-Meiningen, Queen (wife of William IV) 160, 206

Adolphus of Teck, Marquess of Cambridge (d. 1927: father-in-law of George V) 210-11

Aedh, King of Scots 112

Ælfred, King of Wessex 10, 36-7, 198, 200

Ælfwald I, King of the Northumbrians 28

Ælfwine, Bishop of Winchester (d. 1047) 46, 52, 199-201

Ælgifu, Queen: see Emma

Ælla, King of Deira 26

Æscwine, King of Wessex 30

Æthelbald, King of Mercia 23-4

Æthelbald, King of Wessex 32-3

Æthelbert I, King of Kent 21, 151, 180

Æthelbert II, King of Kent 22

Æthelbert, King of Wessex 33-4

Æthelfrith, King of Bernicia 26-7

Æthelheard, King of Wessex 30-1

Æthelred I, King of the Northumbrians 29

Æthelred I, King of Wessex 34-5

Æthelred II, King of England 4, 12, 44, 47, 151, 195, 200

Æthelred, King of Mercia 22

Æthelstan, King of Wessex 37-8, 200

Æthelwald, Prince (son of Æthelred I) 37

Æthelwealh, King of Sussex 30

Æthelweard, Abbot 41

Æthelwulf, King of Wessex 29, 32-3, 36, 199-201

Aidan, St (d. 651) 26

Albany, Duke of: see Leopold

Albert of Saxe-Coburg Gotha, Prince Consort (husband of Victoria) 143-5, 160, 205, 207-8, 210-11

Albert Victor, Duke of Clarence (1864–1892, son of Edward VII) 205, 208

Albrecht, Duke of Bavaria (1905–1996) 163

Aldfrith, King of the Northumbrians 27-8

Alexander I, King of Scots 114, 158

Alexander II, King of Scots 119-20, 158

Alexander III, King of Scots 120-1, 158, 173

Alexandra of Denmark, Queen (wife of Edward VII) 145-6, 160-1, 205

Alfonso, Prince (d. 1284: son of Edward I) 191

Alfred, Prince (son of George II) 192

Alfred, Prince (d. 1787: son of George III) 206

Alfred: see also Ælfred

Alice, Grand Duchess of Hesse (1843–1878: daughter of Victoria) 210-11

Alice of Albany, Countess of Athlone (1883–1981: granddaughter of Victoria) 210-11

235

Amelia, Princess (d. 1786: daughter of George II) 192
Amelia, Princess (1783–1810: daughter of George III) 206
Amesbury, Abbey Church 153
Andechs, Germany, Klosterkirche & Friedhof 164
Andrews, Rev. G.T. 72
Angers, France, Cathedral Church of St Maurice 155; Church of St Denis-le-Frenoit 52
Anna Sophia, Princess (d. 1686: daughter of Anne) 192-3
Annabella Drummond, Queen (wife of Robert III) 158
Anne, Queen of Great Britain 92, 105, 108-9, 192-3
Anne of Bohemia, Queen (wife of Richard II) 71-2, 154, 191
Anne of Cleves, Queen (wife of Henry VIII) 156
Anne of Denmark, Queen (wife of James VI & I) 98, 157, 192-3
Anne Boleyn, Queen (wife of Henry VIII) 94, 96, 156
Anne Neville, Queen (wife of Richard III) 156, 191
Antony, Duc de Montpensier (d. 1807: brother of Louis Philippe of France) 192-3
Arbroath, Angus, Abbey Church of the Virgin Mary and St Thomas à Becket 10, 118-19, 167
Argyll, Duke of: see Campbell
Arthur (legendary king) 39-40
Arthur, Duke of Connaught (1850–1942: son of Victoria) 210-11
Arthur, Prince of Wales (1486–1502: son of Henry VII) 60
Arthur of Connaught, Prince (1883–1938: grandson of Victoria) 210-11
Arundel Castle 20
Athlone, Countess of: see Alice of Albany
Athlone, Earl of: see Cambridge
Augusta, Duchess of Brunswick (d. 1813: daughter of George II) 206

Augusta, Princess of Wales (d. 1772: daughter-in-law of George II) 192
Augusta Sophia, Princess (1768–1840: daughter of George III) 206
Ayloffe, Sir Joseph (1709–1781) 72
Aynburg 29

Baigent, Francis Joseph 201
Balleiul, France, Church of St Waast 120-1
Balliol: see **Edward**; **John**
Balmerino Abbey, Fife 158
Bamborough 26
Bardney Abbey, Lincolnshire 22, 26
Basingwerk 23
Beaufort, Joan: see Joan Beaufort, Queen
Beaufort, John, Duke of Somerset (1403–1444: grandson of Edward III) 34
Beaufort, Margaret, Countess of Richmond & Derby (d. 1509: mother of Henry VII) 34, 192-3
Bec, Normandy, France, Abbaye de 54, 56, 167
Bedford 23
Bedford, Duke of: see John of Lancaster
Bélem, Lisbon, Portugal, Mosteiro dos Jerónimos 157
Bellomonte, Ermengarde de: see Ermengarde de Bellomonte, Queen
Beorhric, King of Wessex 31
Berengaria of Navarre, Queen (wife of Richard I) 152
Bergen, Kristkirken Cathedral 120
Berkeley Castle, Gloucestershire 67
Bertha, Queen (wife of Æthelbert I of Kent) 151
Birinus, St, Bishop 200
Blanche of the Tower, Princess (d. 1342: daughter of Edward III) 191
Blois, Abbaye de St Laumer 154
Bohun, Hugh de (d. 1304: grandson of Edward I) 71, 191
Bohun, Mary de (d. 1305: granddaughter of Edward I) 71, 191
Bohun, Mary de, Duchess of Lancaster (wife of Henry IV before accession) 155

Boleyn, Anne: see Anne Boleyn, Queen
Bosham, Sussex, Holy Trinity Church 49, 167
Bosworth Field, Leicestershire 84
Bothganowan, Elgin 113
Bourchier, Elizabeth, Protectress (wife of Oliver Cromwell) 157
Bowes-Lyon, Elizabeth: see Elizabeth Bowes-Lyon, Queen
Bowker, Alfred 37
Bracci, Pietro (1700–1773) 162
Bradford-on-Avon, Wiltshire 42
Bristol, Abbey 67
Broedericsworth: see Bury St Edmunds
Broker, Nicholas 71
Brookwood, Surrey 43
Brothwell, Don 42
Bruce, Lady Louisa 124
Bruce, Marjory, Princess (daughter of Robert I) 127
Bruce, Thomas, 7th Earl of Elgin (1766–1841) 124
Bruce, Victor Alexander, 9th Earl of Elgin (1849–1917) 124, 158
Bruce-Mitford, Rupert 18
Buckingham, Dukes of: see Villiers
Buckinghamshire, Dukes of 192-3; see Sheffield
Burgh, Elizabeth de: see Elizabeth de Burgh, Queen
Burgh-on-the-Sands, Cumbria 64
Burhed, King of Mercia 25
Bury St Edmunds 19, 44
Butler, James, Duke of Ormonde (1610–1688) 101, 192-3

Cædwalla, King of Wessex 30
Caen, France, Abbaye de le Trinité 151-2; Abbaye de St Etienne 50, 53, 167-8
Cambridge, Alexander, Earl of Athlone (1874–1957: brother-in-law of George V) 210-11
Cambridge, Duke of: see Charles
Cambridge, George, Marquess of Cambridge (d. 1981: nephew of George V) 210-11
Cambridge, Lady May (1906–1994:

great-granddaughter of Victoria) 210-11
Cambridge, Marquess of: see Adolphus of Teck
Cambridge, Rupert, Viscount Trematon (1907-1928: great-grandson of Victoria) 209-11
Cambridge, Sidney Sussex College 102-3
Cambuskenneth, Stirlingshire, Abbey Church of St Mary 130-1, 158, 168-9
Campbell, Archibald, Duke of Argyll (1682–1761) 192-3
Campbell, Caroline, Countess of Dalkeith (d. 1791) 192-3
Canova, Antonio (1767–1822) 163
Canterbury, Kent, Abbey Church of St Augustine 21, 22, 151, 168-70; Cathedral of Christ Church 73-4, 153, 155, 170-1
Cardross Castle, Renfrewshire 121
Carlisle 116
Carlo Emanuele IV, King of Sardinia (1751–1819) 163
Caroline of Brandenburg-Anspach, Queen (wife of George II) 5, 138, 140, 160, 192
Caroline of Brunswick (wife of George IV) 160
Caroline Augusta Matilda, Princess (d. 1775) 205
Caroline Elizabeth (d. 1757: daughter of George II) 192
Carter, Phyllis 187
Carteret, Grace, Countess Granville (d. 1744) 192-3
Carteret, John, Earl Granville (1690–1763) 192-3
Carteret, Lady Frances (d. 1743) 192-3
Carteret, Sophia, Countess Granville (d. 1745) 192-3
Castle Galliard, France 120
Castle Rising, Lincolnshire 154
Catherine of Aragon, Queen (wife of Henry VIII) 81, 89, 91, 94, 156
Catherine of Braganza, Queen (wife of Charles II) 157
Catherine of Valois, Queen (wife of Henry V) 2, 76, 155, 191

Catherine Howard, Queen (wife of Henry VIII) 94, 156
Catherine Parr, Queen (wife of Henry VIII) 91, 156
Cenelm (St), King of Mercia 25
Cenewalh, King of Wessex 29, 30, 196
Centwine, King of Wessex 30
Ceolred, King of Mercia 22
Ceolwulf (St), King of the Northumbrians 28
Ceolwulf, King of Wessex 30
Chaillot, France, Convent of the Visitandine Nuns 107, 157
Chalus, France 57, 60
Charlemagne, Holy Roman Emperor 23, 31
Charles I, King of Scots & England 4, 92, 98, 101, 157, 174, 208
Charles II, King of Scots & England 4, 10, 100-1, 105-6, 108-9, 174, 192-3
Charles 'III', Count of Albany (1720–1788) 108, 162-3
Charles V, King of France (1364–1380) 187
Charles, Duke of Cambridge (d. 1661: son of James VII & II) 192-3
Charles, Duke of Cambridge (d. 1677: son of James VII & II) 192-3
Charles, Duke of Kendale (d. 1677: son of James VII & II) 192-3
Charlotte of Mecklenburg-Strelitz, Queen (wife of George III) 160, 206
Charlotte Augusta, Princess (1796-1817: daughter of George IV) 139, 165, 205-6
Chertsey, Surrey, Abbey Church of St Peter 76, 78-9, 170, 172
Chinon, France 56
Chislehurst, Kent, St Mary's Catholic Church 165
Christian of Schleswig-Holstein (d. 1917: son-in-law of Victoria) 210-11
Clarence, Dukes of: see Albert Victor; Lionel
Claridge, Frances 187
Claridge, Geoffrey 43
Claridge, John Wilson (1905-1993) 42-3

Claypole, Elizabeth (d. 1658: daughter of Oliver Cromwell) 192
Cnut, King of England & Denmark 6, 19, 45-7, 52, 151, 199-201
Coenred, King of Mercia 22
Coenwulf, King of Mercia 23, 25
Coke, Mary, Vicecountess Coke (d. 1810) 192-3
Colt, M. 98
Connaught, Duke of: see Arthur
Constantine I, King of Scots 111-12
Constantine II, King of Scots 112-13
Constantine III, King of Scots 113
Constantine the Great, Roman Emperor 124
Constantinople, Turkey, Nur-i Osmaniye Mosque 124
Corfe Castle, Dorset 41
Cornwall, Earl of: see John of Eltham
Cox, James 102
Craggs, James (d. 1720) 192-3
Cranch, James 102
Critz, J. de 98
Cromwell, Elizabeth 102, 104
Cromwell, Mary, Countess Fauconburg 102
Cromwell, Oliver 1, 4-5, 9, 12, 100-2, 157, 192-3
Cromwell, Richard 102, 104-5, 157
Culen, King of Scots 113
Cumberland, Dukes of: see Henry Fredrick; Rupert; William Augustus
Cuthbert, St 26, 28
Cuthred II, King of Wessex 31
Cynegils, King of Wessex 29-30, 32-3, 199, 200-1
Cyneheard, Prince, son of Sigeberht 31
Cynewulf, King of Wessex 31-2, 199-201

Darnley, James (d. 1686: illegitimate son of James VII & II) 192-3
Darnley, Lord: see Henry Stewart
David I, King of Scots 116, 120, 158, 168, 173, 182
David II, King of Scots 121, 126
Destailleur, Gabriel 165
Deville, Achille 59
Dick, Sir William Reid (1878–1961) 148-9

Dines, George 145
Donald I, King of Scots 111-12
Donald II, King of Scots 112
Donald III, King of Scots 115-16
Douai, France, Scots' College 157
Douglas, Sir James (1286–1330) 121
Douglas, Margaret, Countess of Lennox
    (d. 1578: grandmother of James VI &
    I) 192-3
Dowding, Hugh, Baron Dowding
    (1882–1970) 192-3
Drummond, Annabella: see Annabella
    Drummond, Queen
Dubh, King of Scots 113
Dudley, Lord Guilford (husband of
    Jane) 156
Duncan I, King of Scots 113-14
Duncan II, King of Scots 115-16, 172
Dundee 116
Dundonald Castle, Ayrshire 127
Dundurn, Perthshire 112
Dunfermline, Fife, Abbey Church of the
    Holy Trinity 1, 114-17, 120-5, 157-8,
    172-3
Dunkeld 116
Dunnichen 21
Dunottar 112
Durham, Cathedral Church of St
    Cuthbert 26, 28

Eadbald, King of Kent 22
Eadberht, King of the Northumbrians 28
Eadred, King of Wessex 40, 200-1
Ealhmund, Under-King of Kent 31
Earconbert, King of Kent 22
Ecgbriht I, King of Kent 22, 170
Ecgfrith, King of the Northumbrians 27
Ed-: see also Ead-
Edgar, King of Scots 116
Edgar, King of Wessex and England 37,
    40-1, 170, 200
Edgar, Duke of Richmond (1671: son of
    James VII & II) 192-3
Edinburgh 116, 126; Abbey of Holyrood
    3, 126, 130, 132-3, 158-9, 173-5; St
    Margaret's Convent 64; Trinity
    Church, 158

Edith, Queen (wife of Edward the
    Confessor) 151
Edmund (St), King of East Anglia 18-20,
    44
Edmund I, King of Wessex 37, 39-40, 151
Edmund II Ironside, King of Wessex 39,
    44-5
Edmund, King of Scots 116
Edmund of Langley, Duke of York
    (1341–1402: son of Edward III) 69,
    179-80
Edmund, Earl of Lancaster (1245–1296:
    son of Henry III) 191
Edmund, Prince, son of Ælfred 201
Edward Augustus, Duke of York (son
    of George II) 192
Edward the Confessor, King of
    England 47-50, 62, 65, 68, 76, 151,
    187-8, 190-1, 200
Edward the Elder, King of Wessex 36-7,
    198, 200
Edward the Martyr, King of England
    41-2
Edward I, King of England 48, 62, 64-7,
    120-1, 153-4, 180, 191
Edward II, King of England 12, 67-8,
    121, 154, 177-9, 182
Edward III, King of England 11, 67-71,
    73, 86, 126, 154, 180, 191, 202
Edward IV, King of England 5, 11-12,
    14, 76, 151, 187-8, 190-1, 200, 205
Edward V, King of England 83-4, 192-3
Edward VI, King of England 12, 92-4,
    192
Edward VII, King of Great Britain 14-15,
    72, 100, 145-6, 160, 205
Edward VIII, King of Great Britain, later
    Duke of Windsor 1, 148
Edward Balliol, King of Scotland 126
Edward, Duke of Kent (d. 1820: son of
    George III) 143, 206, 210-11
Edward, Prince (d. 1093: son of
    Malcolm III) 114
Edward, Prince of Wales (the 'Black
    Prince', 1330–1376: son of Edward
    III) 67, 69,71, 73, 171
Edward, Prince of Wales (1453–1471:
    son of Henry VI) 130

Edwin, King of the Northumbrians 26
Edwy, King of England 40
Egbert, King of Wessex 31-2, 199-201
Egfrith, King of Mercia 23
Egilfu, Queen (wife of Edmund I) 151
Eleanor of Aquitaine, Queen (wife of
    Henry II) 57, 152-3, 175
Eleanor of Castille, Queen (wife of
    Edward I) 153-4, 191
Eleanor of Provence, Queen (wife of
    Henry III) 153
Eleanor, Duchess of Gloucester (d. 1399:
    daughter-in-law of Edward III) 191
Eleanor, Princess (daughter of Edward
    I) 191
Elf-: see Ælf-
Elgin, Earls of: see Bruce
Elizabeth I, Queen of England 12-13,
    91-2, 94-8, 135, 188, 192-3, 208
Elizabeth II, Queen of Great Britain 149
Elizabeth, Princess (d. 1495: daughter of
    Henry VII) 191
Elizabeth, Queen of Bohemia
    (1596–1662: daughter of James VI &
    I) 192-3
Elizabeth of York, Queen (wife of
    Henry VII) 86-7, 89, 98-9, 156, 192
Elizabeth Bowes-Lyon, Queen (wife of
    George VI) 149-50, 161, 205
Elizabeth de Burgh, Queen (wife of
    Robert I) 158
Elizabeth Woodville, Queen (wife of
    Edward IV) 83, 155, 205
Elizabeth Caroline, Princess (d. 1759:
    granddaughter of George II) 192
embalming procedures 5-9, 140
Emlyn, Henry (1729–1815) 78, 83, 207
Emma, Ælgifu, Queen (wife of Æthelred
    II & Cnut) 46, 52, 151, 199-200
Eochaid, King of Scots 112
Eowa (nephew of Penda) 23
Erik II, King of Norway 120
Ermengarde de Bellomonte, Queen
    (wife of William the Lion) 158
Ernst I, Duke of Saxe-Coburg & Gotha
    (1784–1844) 145
Ernst August, Duke of Brunswick
    (1882–1953) 138

Ernst August, Elector of Hanover
    (1629–1690) 138
Ernst August, King of Hanover
    (1771–1851) 138
Ethel-: see Æthel-
Eugénie, Empress of the French 165
Euphemia Ross, Queen (wife of Robert
    II) 158
Eustace, Prince (son of Stephen) 54

Falkland, Fife 132
Fårevejle Church, Denmark 159-60
Farnborough, St Michael's Abbey 165
Farndon-on-Dee 37
Faversham, Kent, Abbey Church of Our
    Saviour 10, 54-5, 175; Church of St
    Mary of Charity 54, 151
Felipe II, King of Spain 114, 156-7
Fetteresso, Kincardineshire 112
Fitzcharles, Charles, Earl of Plymouth
    (1657–1680: illegitimate son of
    Charles II) 192-3
Fitzgerald, John, Earl of Kildare (d.
    1707) 192-3
Fitzgerald, Mary, Countess of Kildare
    (d. 1683) 192-3
Fitzroy, George, Duke of
    Northumberland (1665–1716:
    illegitimate son of Charles II) 192-3
Flitcroft, Henry 140
Flodden Field, Northumberland 131
Fontevraud (Fontévrault), France,
    Abbaye de 56-60, 62-3, 151-3, 175-6
Fordoun, Kincardineshire 112
Forres, Morayshire 112-13
Fotheringhay Castle, Lincolnshire 132
Fox, Richard, Bishop of Winchester (d.
    1528) 200
Frances, Duchess of Suffolk (d. 1559:
    mother of Jane) 191
Francesco V, Duke of Modena
    (1819–1875) 164
Francis of Teck (d. 1910: brother-in-law
    of George V) 209-11
Francis, Duke of Teck (d. 1900:
    father-in-law of George V) 206
François II, King of France 132, 159
Frascati, Basilica of San Pietro 162

Frederick Augustus, Duke of York
(1763–1827: son of George III) 206
Frederick Lewis, Prince of Wales
(1707–1751: son of George II) 192
Frederick William, Prince (grandson of
George II) 192
Friederike, Queen of Hanover
(1778–1841) 138
Frytheswyda, Queen of Mercia 151
Frytheswyda, St 151

Gainsborough, Lincolnshire 44
Gaveston, Piers (d. 1312) 179
Gent, Flanders, Church of St Bavon 92
Geoffrey V, Duke of Anjou 151
Georg V, King of Hanover 138, 165-6,
206-7
George I, King of Great Britain 137-8,
160
George II, King of Great Britain 5, 12,
138-40, 160, 192
George III, King of Great Britain 1, 10,
12, 92, 140-2, 160, 163, 204, 206-8
George IV, King of Great Britain 10, 14,
100, 108, 139-40, 142, 160, 163, 206
George V, King of Great Britain 146-8,
161, 205
George VI, King of Great Britain 1, 15,
148-50, 161, 163, 205, 207
George, Duke of Kent (1902–1942: son
of George V) 209-11
George, Prince (d. 1479: son of Edward
IV) 205
George, Prince (son of Anne) 192-3
George, Prince (son of George II) 192
George of Denmark, Prince (husband of
Anne) 105, 157, 192-3
Gillis, Bishop James (1802–1864) 64, 114
Giric I, King of Scots 112
Giric II, King of Scots 113
Glamis, Angus 113
Glastonbury, Abbey Church 39, 40-1,
44, 175, 177
Gloucester 40; Cathedral Church of St
Peter 67, 177-8; Priory Church of St
Oswald 26, 179
Gloucester, Duchesses of: see Eleanor;
Mary

Gloucester, Dukes of: see Henry;
Thomas; William; William Frederick;
William Henry
Granville, Earl of: see Carteret
Greenwich Palace 92
Grosvenor, Margaret, Marchioness of
Cambridge (d. 1929: sister-in-law of
George V) 210-11
Guinevere, legendary queen 40
Gytha 49

Halford, Sir Henry (1866–1844) 100
Halifax, Marquess of: see Saville
Hamilton, Catherine, Duchess of
Abercorn (d. 1723) 192-3
Hamilton, Charles, Earl of Selkirk (d.
1738) 192-3
Hanover, Herrenhausen 138;
Leineschloss 137-8
Harold I, King of England 45
Harold II, King of England 49-50
Harthacnut, King of England 46-7, 200
Hawksmoor, Nicholas (1661–1736) 188
heart burial 9, 57
Heathcote, Sir William 105
Helena, Princess Christian of
Schleswig-Holstein (d. 1923:
daughter of Victoria) 206, 210-11
Henrietta, Princess (d. 1669: daughter of
James VII & II) 192-3
Henrietta Anne, Duchess of Orleans
(1644–1670: daughter of Charles I)
163
Henrietta Maria of France, Queen (wife
of Charles I) 105, 157
Helena Victoria of Schleswig-Holstein,
Princess (1870–1948: granddaughter
of Victoria) 210-11
Henry 'the Young King' (1155–1183) 187
Henry I, King of England 10, 47, 52-4,
151, 180, 184, 198
Henry II, King of England 47, 56-7, 60,
64, 152-3, 175
Henry III, King of England 21, 47-8,
62-4, 76, 86, 151, 153, 175, 180, 188,
191, 202, 207
Henry IV, King of England 71, 73-4, 155,
171

Henry V, King of England 2, 11, 14, 56, 72, 74-7, 131, 154-5, 191

Henry VI, King of England 14-15, 76-9, 86, 89, 145, 155, 205, 207

Henry VII, King of England 5, 10, 12, 83-9, 94, 98-9, 140, 155-6, 188, 192, 202, 207

Henry VIII, King of England 4, 12, 49, 60, 81, 89-92, 94, 96, 99-100, 131, 140, 156, 172, 180, 204, 208

Henry 'I & IX', Cardinal Duke of York 108, 162-3

Henry of Blois, Bishop (1129–1171) 198, 201

Henry, Duke of Gloucester (1640–1660: son of Charles I) 192-3

Henry, Duke of Gloucester (1900–1974: son of George V) 210-11

Henry, Prince (son of Edward I) 191

Henry, Prince of Wales (d. 1612: son James VI & I) 192-3

Henry Stewart, Lord Darnley 52, 98, 132, 159, 174-5

Henry Fredrick, Duke of Cumberland (1745–1790: grandson of George II) 140, 192

Hepburn, James, Earl of Bothwell 132, 159

Herrick, Robert, Mayor of Leicester 85

Hesse, Grand Duchess of: see Alice

Hexham Abbey 28

Hild, Abbess 195

Hinsley, Arthur, Cardinal Archbishop of Westminster (1865–1943) 163

Hlothere, King of Kent 22

Holland, Margaret, Duchess of Beaufort & Clarence 34

Horsey, Sir John 187

Howard, Catherine: see Catherine Howard

Howard, Henry 201

Humbert, Albert Jenkins 145

Hursley, Hampshire, All Saint's Church 102, 104-5

Hyde, Anne, Duchess of York (wife of James VII & II prior to his accession) 157, 192-3

Hylton, Walter 85

Ina, King of Wessex 30, 175

Indulf, King of Scots 113

Invercullen 113

Iona 1, 27, 111-14, 116, 179

Isabel of Valois, Queen (wife of Richard II) 154

Isabella, Princess (d. 1680: daughter of James VII & II) 192-3

Isabella of Angoulême, Queen (wife of John) 57, 153

Isabella of France, Queen (wife of Edward II) 67

Isabella of Gloucester, Queen (wife of John) 153

James I, King of England: see James VI & I

James I, King of Scots 10, 127, 129-30, 158, 184

James II, King of England: see James VII & II

James II, King of Scots 130, 158

James III, King of Scots 130-1, 158

James IV, King of Scots 131-2, 159

James V, King of Scots 94, 132-3, 159, 173-4

James VI & I, King of Scots & England 5, 10, 12, 13, 97-9, 132, 135, 137, 156-7, 174, 184, 192

James VII & II, King of Scots and England 106-8, 159, 162-3, 174, 208

James 'VIII & III', Prince of Wales (son of James VII & II) 106-8, 162-3

James, Duke of Cambridge (d. 1667: son of James VII & II) 192-3

James, John 188

Jane, Queen of England 94, 156

Jane Seymour, Queen (wife of Henry VIII) 90-2, 156

Janyns, Henry 202

Jedborough 116

Joan of England, Queen (wife of Alexander II) 158

Joan of Navarre, Queen (wife of Henry IV) 73-4, 155

Joan of the Tower, Princess (daughter of Edward III) 69

Joan Beaufort, Queen (wife of James I) 129, 158, 184

Joan Plantagenet, Countess of Toulouse 57

Johann Friedrich, Duke of Hanover (1625–1679) 138

John, King of England 60-2, 153, 175

John Balliol, King of Scotland 120-1

John, Prince (son of Edward I) 191

John, Prince (son of Henry III) 191

John of Eltham, Earl of Cornwall (1316–1336: son of Edward II) 191

John of Gaunt, Duke of Lancaster (son of Edward III) 73

John of Lancaster, Duke of Bedford (1389–1435: son of Henry IV) 187

John of Liège 68

Jones, Inigo (1573–1652) 180

Karl II, Duke of Brunswick-Wolfenbüttel (1735–1806) 160

Katherine, Princess (d. 1257: daughter of Henry III) 191

Katherine, Princess (d. 1671: daughter of James VII & II) 192-3

Katherine Laura, Princess (d. 1675: daughter of James VII & II) 192-3

Keble, Rev John (1792–1866) 105

Kendale, Duke of: see Charles

Kenneth I, King of Scots 111

Kenneth II, King of Scots 113

Kenneth III, King of Scots 113-14

Kensington Palace 108, 138

Kent, Dukes of: see Edward, George

Kildare, Earl of: see Fitzgerald

King, Edward (1735–1807) 72

Kinghorn, Fife 120

King's Langley, Hertfordshire, Priory Church of the House of the Friars Preachers 72, 179-80

Kitchin, George, Dean of Winchester (1827–1912) 201

Knox, John (1505–1572) 174, 184

Labilliere, Dean 140

Lancaster, Dukes of: see Henry IV; John of Gaunt (son of Edward III) 73

Le Mans, Cathedral of St Julien 151-3

Leicester, Abbey Church of St Mary 180; Grey Friars Abbey 85

Lennox, Charles, Duke of Richmond (d. 1723: illegitimate son of Charles II) 192-3

Lennox, Earls & Countesses of: see Douglas; Stuart

Leominster 42

Leopold, Duke of Albany (1853–1884: son of Victoria) 205, 207

L'Epau, France Abbaye de 152-3

Lichfield 22; Cathedral 153

Lindisfarne 26, 28-9

Lionel, Duke of Clarence (1338–1368: son of Edward III) 69

Lisbon, Portugal, Church of São Vicente De Fora 157

Little Driffield, Yorkshire 28

London, Buckingham Palace 145; Christ Church, Newgate 154; Church of St Clement Danes 45; Church of St Gregory the Great 19; Church of St Michael, Wood Street 132; Church of the Franciscans 153; Church of the Grey Friars, Newgate 67, 154; Monastery of the Blackfriars 153; St Paul's Cathedral 21, 44, 92, 100, 180-1; Tower of London 76; Chapel of St Peter ad Vincula 94, 156, 180

Lote, Stephen 71

Louis, King of England: see Louis VIII

Louis VIII, King of France 61-2

Louis IX, King of France 59

Louis-Philippe, King of the French 57

Louisa Anne Princess (d. 1751: daughter of George II) 192

Louise, Duchess of Argyll (1848–1939: daughter of Victoria) 210-11

Louise, Duchess of Connaught (d. 1917: daughter-in-law of Victoria) 210-11

Lulach, King of Scots 114

Lutyens, Sir Edwin (1869–1944) 147

Macbeth, King of Scots 113-14

Mackennal, Sir Bertram (1863–1931) 145

Madeleine de Valois, Queen (wife of James V) 159, 174-5

Madrid, Real Monasterio de San Lorenzo de El Escorial 114, 156-7

Maidestone, Clement 73

Maijor, Dorothy (wife of Richard Cromwell) 157

Malcolm I, King of Scots 112-13

Malcolm II, King of Scots 113-14, 116

Malcolm III, King of Scots 114-16, 157-8

Malcolm IV, King of Scots 116, 172

Malmesbury, Abbey Church of SS Peter, Paul, Aldhelm and Mary 37-8, 67, 180, 182

Malpei, Mormaer of the Mearns 116

Margaret, Queen of Scots 120

Margaret, Countess of Snowdon (daughter of George VI) 149, 205

Margaret, Princess (d. 1472: daughter of Edward IV) 191

Margaret, Princess (daughter of Edward IV) 11

Margaret, Queen of Norway (daughter of Alexander III) 120

Margaret of Anjou, Queen (wife of Henry VI) 79, 130 155

Margaret of Denmark, Queen (wife of James III) 158-9

Margaret of England, Queen (wife of Alexander III) 158

Margaret of France, Queen (wife of Edward I) 154

Margaret Atheling (St), Queen (wife of Malcolm III) 114-15, 120, 157-8, 172-3

Margaret Tudor, Queen (wife of James IV) 159, 184

Maria, Duchess of Gloucester (d. 1807) 205

Maria Beatrice of Savoy, Duchess of Modena (1792–1840) 164

Maria Theresa of Austria-Este, Queen of Bavaria (1849–1919) 164

Marie, Queen of Yugoslavia (d. 1961: wife of Alexander I of Yugoslavia) 210-11

Marie Louise of Schleswig-Holstein, Princess (1872–1956: granddaughter of Victoria) 210-11

Marina of Greece, Duchess of Kent (1906–1968: daughter-in-law of George V) 209-11

Marochetti, Baron Carlo 145

Martin, Hampshire 34

Mary I, Queen of England 47, 92, 94-8, 156, 188, 192-3

Mary II, Queen of Scots & of England 9, 105, 108-9, 192-3

Mary, Queen of Scots 5, 12-13, 98, 132, 134-5, 159-60, 192-3

Mary, Duchess of Gloucester (1776–1857: daughter of George III) 205

Mary, Princess (d. 1482: daughter of Edward IV) 205

Mary, Princess (d. 1607: daughter of James VI & I) 192-3

Mary, Princess (d. 1686 – daughter of Anne) 192-3

Mary, Princess (daughter of Anne) 192-3

Mary, Princess of Orange (1631–1660: mother of William III & II) 192-3

Mary of Brittany, Princess (daughter of Edward III) 69

Mary of Gueldres, Queen (wife of James II) 158, 175

Mary of Guise, Queen (wife of James V) 159

Mary of Modena, Queen (wife of James VII & II) 157

Mary of Teck, Queen (wife of George V) 147-8, 161, 205

Mary Adelaide, Duchess of Teck (d. 1897: mother-in-law of George V) 206

Mathilda (Maud), Empress of the Romans and Lady of England 54, 56, 151

Matilda (Maud; Mahalde; Mold) of Scotland, Queen (wife of Henry I) 151

Matilda of Boulogne, Queen (wife of Stephen) 151

Matilda of Flanders, Queen (wife of William I) 151

Matilda of Huntingdon, Queen (wife of David I) 158

Maurice of Battenburg, Prince (d. 1914) 210-11

Mellor, John 37

Melrose, Roxburghshire, Abbey Church 119-21, 126, 182-4
Modena, Church of San Vincenzo 164
Monck, Elizabeth, Duchess of Albemarle (d. 1734) 192-3
Monck, George, Duke of Albemarle (1608–1670) 96, 106, 192-3
Mondynes, Kincardineshire 116
Monmouth, Duke of: see Scott
Montagu-Douglas-Scott, Alice, Duchess of Gloucester (1901-2004) 210-11
Montague, Charles, Earl of Halifax (d. 1715) 192-3
Monzievaird, Perthshire 113
Morant, Geoffrey Miles (1899–1964) 102
Mountbatten, Lord Leopold (d. 1922: grandson of Victoria) 210-11
Mowbray, Robert de, Earl of Northumberland (d. 1125?) 114, 187-8
Mowlem, Messrs. 149
Munich 164

Napoleon III, Emperor of the French 57, 156
Napoléon, Prince Imperial 205
Nelson, Horatio, Viscount Nelson (1758–1805) 92
Neville, Anne: see Anne Neville, Queen
Newark, Lincolnshire 60
Newburgh Priory, North Yorkshire 102
Norham-on-Tweed 28
Northborough, Northants, St Andrew's Church 157
Northumberland, Dukes of: see Fitzroy; Percy
Northumberland, Earl of: see Mowbray, Robert de
Nutt, A.Y. 100

Octavius, Prince (d. 1783: son of George III) 206
Offa, King of East Anglia 18
Offa, King of Mercia 23, 31
Orleans, France 64
Orleans, Duchess of: see Henrietta Anne
Osbald, King of the Northumbrians 29
Osred II, King of the Northumbrians 29

Osthryth, Queen of Mercia 26
Oswald (St), King of the Northumbrians 26-7
Oswine, King of Deira 26-7
Oswiu, King of the Northumbrians 27, 195
Oswulf, King of the Northumbrians 28
Otto the Goldsmith 50

Pace, George 149
Paget, Paul 149
Paisley, Renfrewshire, Abbey Church 127, 158, 182-4
Palmerston, Viscount: see Temple
Paris 76; Basilica of St Denis 62, 157, 159; Bois de Boulogne 148; Convent of the English Benedictines 106; Scots' College 107
Parr, Catherine: see Catherine Parr, Queen
Pearson, Karl (1857–1936) 102
Penda, King of Mercia 22-3, 26, 195
Percy, Mary, Duchess of Northumberland (d. 1738) 192-3
Perth, Perthshire 127-9; Charterhouse of the Carthusians 10, 129, 158, 184; Church of St John 129, 159
Peterborough Cathedral 135, 156
Philippa of Hainault, Queen (wife of Edward III) 154, 191
Philippa, Duchess of York (d. 1431: granddaughter-in-law of Edward III) 191
Philippe II, King of France 61
Phillips, Charles 18
Pius IX, Pope (1792–1878) 114
Pius XI, Pope (1857–1939) 163
Plymouth, Earl of: see Fitzcharles
Prest, Godfrey 71
Pretty, Edith 19
Prince Consort: see Albert of Saxe-Coburg Gotha
Prittlewell, Southend 20-3
Puy, Claudius Du 102

Rædwald, King of East Anglia 17-18
Ramsay, Sir Alexander (d. 1972: grandson-in-law of Victoria) 210-11

Ramsay, Lady Patricia (1886–1974: granddaughter of Victoria) 210-11
Rathinveramon 113
Raymond VII, Count of Toulouse 56-7
Reading, Berkshire, Abbey Church of Virgin Mary and St John the Evangelist 10, 53-4, 154, 184
Reculver, Kent 22
Reims, Cathedral 159
Repton, Derbyshire, Church of St Wystan 23-5, 184-5
Rescobie, Forfarshire 116
Rhiderch, King of Strathclyde 113
Richard I, King of England 57-60, 152-3, 187
Richard II, King of England 11, 66, 71-3, 154, 179, 182, 191
Richard III, King of England 78, 83-6, 156
Richard, Duke of York (1472–1483?: son of Edward IV) 83-4, 192-3
Richard, Prince (son of Henry III) 191
Richmond, Duke of: see Stuart
Richmond, Dukes of 192-3
Richmond, Dukes of: see Edgar; Edward; Edward Augustus
Richmond, Dukes of: see Lennox
Richmond Palace 86, 96
Rizzello, Michael (1926–2004) 150
Robert I, King of Scots 64, 121-7, 158, 173
Robert II, King of Scots 127, 158
Robert III, King of Scots 127-8, 158
Robert, Duke of Normandy (1054?–1134: son of William I) 52
Rome, Church of St Mary in the English College 22, 25; Church of Sant' Andrea al Quirinale 164; Pontifical Scots College 163
Roskilde Cathedral, Denmark 44
Ross, Euphemia: see Euphemia Ross, Queen
Rothesay Castle, Ayrshire 127
Rouen 54; Cathedral of Notre Dame des Pres 53, 56-9, 76, 184, 186-7
Rovezzano, Benedetto da 89, 94
Rupert, Duke of Cumberland (d. 1682: grandson of Charles I) 192-3

Rupprecht, Crown Prince of Bavaria (1869–1955) 164
Russell, Samuel 102

Saeberht, King of Essex 20-1, 188, 191
Salisbury 42
Sandringham, Norfolk 146, 148
Saville, George, Marquess of Halifax (1633–1695) 192-3
Scone Abbey 127, 158
Scott, Sir George Gilbert (1811–1878) 94, 190
Scott, James, Duke of Monmouth (1649–1685: illegitimate son of Charles II) 192-3
Seaxburh, Queen of Wessex 30
Sebbi, King of Essex 21
Seckington, Staffordshire 23
Selkirk, Earl of: see Hamilton
Seymour, Edward, Earl of Hertford & Duke of Somerset (1506?–1552) 174
Seymour, Jane: see Jane Seymour, Queen
Seymour, R.B. 72
Shaftesbury, Abbey Church of St Mary and St Edward 41-4, 151
Sheen, Surrey 67, 131-2
Sheffield, Catherine, Duchess of Buckinghamshire (d. 1743) 192-3
Sheffield, Edmund, Duke of Buckinghamshire (d. 1735) 192-3
Sheffield, John, Duke of Buckinghamshire (1648–1721) 192-3
Sherborne, Abbey Church of St Mary the Virgin 33-4, 187-8
Sigeberht I, King of Essex 21
Sigeberht, King of Wessex 31
Sighere, King of Essex 21
Sobieska, Clementina 162
Somerset, Dukes of: see Beaufort; Seymour
Sophia, Electress of Hanover (1630–1716) 138, 162
Sophia, Princess (d. 1606: daughter of James VI & I) 192-3
Sophia Dorothea of Brunswick-Lüneburg and Celle, Queen (wife of George I) 160
Sophia Matilda, Princess (d. 1844) 205

Spry, J.H. 73

St Albans, Hertfordshire 23

St Andrews, Fife 112

St Germain-en-Laye, France 106-8

St Omer, France, English Church 107

Stanhope, Lady Elizabeth (d. 1708) 192-3

Stanley, Dean Arthur Penrhyn (1815–1881) 72, 89, 98, 135, 157, 192-3

Stanley, Lady Augusta (d. 1876) 192-3

Stephen, King of England 10, 52-4, 151, 175

Steuart, General William (d. 1726)

Stewart: see also Stuart

Stewart, Arbella (1575–1615: great-granddaughter of James IV) 135, 192-3

Stewart, Charles, Earl of Lennox (grandson of James IV) 192-3

Stothard, Charles (1786–1824) 57

Stowell, T.E.A. 42

Strathallan 112

Stuart: see also Stewart

Stuart, Elizabeth, Duchess of Richmond (d. 1661) 192-3

Stuart, Esme, 5th Duke of Richmond (d. 1660) 192-3

Stuart, Ludovic, 2nd Duke of Richmond (d. 1624) 192-3

Stumpe, William 182

Sudeley Castle, St Mary's Church 91, 156

Suffolk, Duchess of: see Frances

Sutton Hoo, Suffolk 1, 17-18

Sweyn, King of Denmark & England 19, 44-5

Swithun, St (d. 862) 196, 198

Sybilla of England, Queen (wife of Alexander I) 158

Sydenham, Laura 187

Tarrant Crawford, Dorset, Nunnery Church 158

Temple, Henry, Viscount Palmerston (1784–1865) 64

Thirske, John 76

Thomas, Duke of Gloucester (d. 1397: son of Edward III) 191

Torel, William 62

Torregiano, Pietro 89, 94

Toulouse, Basilica of St Sernin 19

Trenchard, Hugh, Viscount Trenchard (1873–1956) 192-3

Tresilian, John 179

Tudor, Margaret: see Margaret Tudor, Queen

Turin, Basilica di Superga 164

Tynemouth, The Priory Church of the Blessed Virgin and St Oswin 27-8, 114-15, 187-8

Vanezis, Peter 124

Vatican, Basiilica of San Pietro 30, 162-3

Vaughan, Herbert Alfred, Cardinal Archbishop of Westminster (1832–1903) 20

Versailles 57

Victoria, Queen of Great Britain 14, 57, 108, 127, 165, 210-11

Victoria, Princess (1868–1935: daughter of Edward VII) 210-11

Victoria of Saxe-Coburg-Saafeld, Duchess of Kent (1786-1861: mother of Victoria) 143

Vienna, Kapuzinerkirche 164

Viktoria Luise, Duchess of Brunswick 138

Villiers, Catherine, Vicountess Grandison (d. 1725) 192-3

Villiers, Lord Francis (d. 1648) 192-3

Villiers, Sir George (d. 1605) 191

Villiers, George, Duke of Buckingham (1592–1628) 192-3

Villiers, George, Duke of Buckingham (1628–1687) 192-3

Villiers, Lady Mary (d. 1632) 191

Villiers, Mary, Duchess of Buckingham (d. 1704) 192-3

Vittorio Emanuele I, King of Sardinia (1759–1824) 164

Walpole, Horace (1717-1797) 67

Waltham Abbey 49, 65

Wareham 31; Church of St Mary 41

Warfield, Wallis, Duchess of Windsor (d. 1986) 148, 210-11

Warmington Grange 25

Westminster, Collegiate (Abbey)

Church of St Peter 1-2, 4-5, 10-12, 20-1, 45, 47-9, 62-7, 67-78, 83-4, 86-9, 92-8, 100-2, 105-6, 134-5, 138-40, 151, 153-7, 160, 188-94; Hall 5, 102; Palace 62, 79

Wheatley, Yorkshire 127

Whitby, Abbey Church 26-7, 195

Whitehall Palace 89, 98

Wiglaf, King of Mercia 25

Wihtred, King of Kent 22

Wildenwart, Germany 164

Wilkinson, Canon 102

Wilkinson, Josiah Henry 102

William I, King of England 49, 50-2, 151

William II, King of England 6, 46, 50-2, 199-201

William III & II, King of England & Scots 105, 108-9, 192-3

William IV, King of Great Britain 10, 14, 138, 142-3, 206

William the Lion, King of Scots 10, 118-19, 158, 167

William, Duke of Gloucester (d. 1700: son of Anne) 192-3

William of Gloucester, Prince (1941–1972 - grandson of George V) 210-11

William of Jumieges 49

William of Windsor, Prince (d. 1348: son of Edward III) 191

William the Steward 182

William Augustus, Duke of Cumberland (1721–1765: son of George II) 192

William Frederick, Duke of Gloucester (1776–1834) 205

William Henry, Duke of Gloucester (1743–1805: son of George II) 205

Wimborne Minster, Dorset, Collegiate Church of St Cuthburga 34, 195

Wina, Bishop of Winchester 46, 52, 199

Winchcombe Abbey 23

Winchester 1; Cathedral Church of the Holy and Undivided Trinity 6, 29-33, 40, 44-7, 52, 151, 196-201; Church of St Bartholemew 37; Hyde Abbey 36-7, 198; 'New Minster' 10, 36, 197-8; 'Old Minster' 29-33, 36, 40, 42, 45, 47, 151, 196-7

Windsor, Berkshire 1, 4, 140, 142; The Queen's Free Chapel of St George 12, 14-15, 78-83, 86, 89-92, 98-100, 139-43, 145-50, 155-6, 160-1, 165-6, 202-8; Frogmore 14, 143-5, 148, 160, 208-11

Windsor, Duchess of: see Warfield

Windsor, Duke of: see Edward VIII

Wolsey, Cardinal Thomas (1475?-1530) 89, 99, 140, 207

Woodville, Elizabeth: see Elizabeth Woodville, Queen

Worcester, Cathedral Church of Christ and the Blessed Virgin Mary 60, 209

Wren, Sir Christopher (1632–1723) 100, 132, 154, 180

Wulfhere, King of Mercia 22

Wystan, St 25, 184

Yevele, Henry 73

York 26, 28-9

York, Dukes of: see Edmund; Frederick Augustus; Henry 'I & IX'; Richard